basic call
to
consciousness

basic call to consciousness

Edited by

ĀKWESĀSNE NOTES

NATIVE VOICES

SUMMERTOWN, TENNESSEE

Cover photograph by Dick Bancroft.
Cover design by Warren Jefferson.
Interior illustrations by Kahionhes (John Fadden).

Native Voices, an imprint of
Book Publishing Company
P. O. Box 99
Summertown, TN 38483
(888) 260-8458

Printed in The United States of America-

19 18 17 16 15   4 5 6 7 8 9

ISBN 10 : 1-57067-159-1
ISBN 13: 978-1-57067-159-3

Basic call to consciousness / edited by Akwesasne notes.-- Rev. ed.
   p. cm.
  Includes bibliographical references.
  ISBN 1-57067-159-1
  1. Iroquois Indians--Politics and government. 2. Speeches, addresses, etc., Iroquois. 3. Iroquois Indians--Government relations. 4. Iroqouis Indians--Social conditions. I. Akwesasne notes.
  E99.I7B23 2004
  323.1'19755--dc22

                        2004005301

Credit pending for photographs on pages 20, 58, 59, 64, 65, 66, 67, 72, 113, and 130.

Contents

Native delegates entering the United Nations headquarters in Geneva. In the words of one delegate: "We may seem small yet—but we represent the aspirations of millions and millions of people—small nations which will be recognized."

Akwesasne Notes Photo: Claus Biegert

Introduction

John Mohawk

It was during the era of the administration of President John F. Kennedy, an era that saw some of the highest tensions between the United States and the Soviet Union, that the issue of civil rights gained traction in American politics and opened the way for the U.S. civil rights legislation of the 1960s.

The Civil Rights Movement reverberated around the world. At about the same time, American Indians began demanding rights of a somewhat different nature. African-Americans had been denied full rights as citizens, were widely segregated in ghettos, had poor access to education or job training, and suffered discriminatory hiring practices. In many places, people would not sell them housing.

American Indian nations, on the other hand, once had owned the entire continent, but had been attacked and/or swindled out of most of their properties and most of the practical rights of nationhood. They demanded "Indian rights," which were much more collective and probably even more unpopular in white America than were the African-American demands. By the late 1960s, however, they were beginning to make headway.

Indian tribes that had treaties guaranteeing them fishing rights in the Pacific Northwest challenged state laws prohibiting Indian fishing in violation of those treaties. The Columbia River became a scene of Indian demonstrations and arrests and eventually led to a court case in which Indian rights were at least somewhat upheld. This led to a backlash movement among some whites who wanted to pass legislation to end treaty rights, and the re-energized Indian movement mobilized to defend treaty rights. There was a historic demonstration at Alcatraz Island, at which

Indians called attention to the centuries of abuses of their rights, and demonstrations in California, Oregon, Minnesota, and other places about land claims.

In 1968 in Minnesota, the American Indian Movement (AIM) was formed. It initially became a force for the rights of urban Indigenous people, but soon it gained national attention. The stated goals of AIM were to defend Indian sovereignty and advance Indian rights causes. Their constituency included people in Indian Country and in urban settings. Richard Oakes, a Mohawk college student, helped organize a demonstration occupation of an abandoned prison complex on Alcatraz Island in northern California. It garnered considerable publicity and became a touchstone for Native activists from across the continent. The occupation began on November 20, 1969, and continued for approximately nineteen months.

Around the country, Indians mounted protests and demonstrations demanding treaty rights and land returns and opposing encroachment by non-Indians on Indian land. Some of these demonstrations reached the Haudenosaunee Country where people opposed non-Indian encroachment on a trailer court at Tuscarora and, more famously, opposed widening a road at Route 81 on the Onondaga Territory. The mood in Indian Country was that there would be no further loss of land, not even a little land for widening a highway.

American Indian Movement activists joined Indian rights activists nationally in raising an alarm that Indian ways were declining and Indian people were generally rendered powerless and in a state of abject poverty, especially on their lands. There was something of a national cultural revitalization and a concurrent complaint that there was a crisis in leadership in Indian Country, because the leaders had become co-opted by the U.S. government and non-Indian culture and could not see or act on Indian interests. Generations of colonization had taken their toll and had left Indian Country with leaders who seemed primarily interested in collecting federal grant money and not in exercising sovereignty. This was a message that came to resonate widely across Indian Country.

In 1972, a wide coalition of activists, including members of the American Indian Movement, organized a march on Washington to protest the treatment of Indians and to urge reforms of the Bureau of Indian Affairs. The event was dubbed the "Trail of Broken Treaties," and hundreds of Indians initially made their way to Washington in October 1972, days before the presidential election. When building security tried to evict the demonstrators while negotiations went on in the main offices, the security forces were driven from the building and an occupation of a federal building in the capital—said to be the first since the War of 1812—ensued. The occupation lasted from November 3 to November 9, but the energy in Indian Country was rising, and during the winter of 1973, a small force of AIM supporters and local activists declared the historic village of Wounded Knee, site of a horrific massacre in 1890, as sovereign territory. The occupiers were surrounded by a military force, and an ensuing standoff lasted seventy-three days and resulted in Indian fatalities due to gunfire.

In 1974, the International Indian Treaty Council (IITC) was organized and held its first national meeting at Wakpala on the Standing Rock Sioux Territory in North Dakota. IITC was organized to provide a platform to pursue the rights of Indigenous peoples under international law. After almost two hundred years, the United States, and most of the other nations of the Western Hemisphere, had failed to give meaningful recognition to the rights of a continued existence as a distinct people to any of the Indigenous peoples. Many who were involved in the Indian rights struggle felt that the nation states were hampered by a phenomenon known as the "tyranny of the majority" and would never be able to recognize even the rights bestowed by treaty. A partial remedy—but only one of many—would be the pursuit of the principles of indigenous rights under international law. It was acknowledged that international law had no enforcement powers, but it was felt that the so-called "civilized" nations of the world were generally embarrassed when their behaviors fell beneath the world standards for the treatment of individuals and peoples, and that the indigenous voice was an important and necessary part of the process of discussion around such principles.

The IITC was one of several groups that approached the NGOs—the Non-Governmental Organizations of the United Nations—with a proposal to explore the creation of a process to recognize the rights of Indigenous nations, peoples, and individuals. It was a historic undertaking. It wasn't until early in 1977, when word reached the Grand Council of the Haudenosaunee, located at Onondaga in central New York, that the NGOs were willing to host a meeting. They had sent forward a request for response papers detailing the economic, legal, and social realities of the various Indigenous nations. Although the Iroquois Confederacy is composed of six member nations—the Mohawk, Oneida, Onondaga, Cayuga, Seneca and Tuscarora—the Confederacy acts as a single nation in response to such international requests.

The call for papers was duly discussed. Three individuals were chosen and each was asked to author one of the papers. When finished, the papers would be presented to the Haudenosaunee Grand Council, which would then make alterations and additions and produce a final draft. I was privileged to be chosen to write one of the papers. When the council reconvened, one of the other two individuals who had an assignment reported he would not be able to finish it. I had already finished the assignment I had, and the Council asked if I would be able to do the second paper. I did. The next meeting the third individual reported that he would be unable to complete his paper, and I was asked to write the third paper. Thus I authored the three position papers that appeared in *Akwesasne Notes* and later in *Basic Call to Consciousness*.

I did not go to Geneva in 1977 because we had a newspaper to run. Daniel Bomberry, the Cayuga-Salish man whose father came from the Grand River Country, attended the meeting and took photographs, many of which appeared in *Akwesasne Notes* and editions of *Basic Call.* José Barreiro, who was coeditor of the *Notes*, wrote an exciting account of some important moments at the meeting. When the meeting was over, and we looked at all the material we had, we realized that we had a small book. *Akwesasne Notes* had long before published a short pamphlet on the life of Deskaheh, the Cayuga chief who had gone to Europe to argue against the British military invasion and occupation and disgraceful overthrow of the traditional government at Grand River in 1924. We added the pamphlet to the other material, and a first edition of *Basic Call to Consciousness* appeared in 1978.

The book, or at least significant parts of it, has been translated into many languages. For me, the most edifying feedback was an account I heard from Indian rights activists who met in Washington, DC, in 1980. An individual approached me and explained that *Basic Call to Consciousness* had been translated into Portuguese, and a group had carried the book to Indian communities across Brazil and had read it to the rainforest Indians. He said these Indians thoroughly enjoyed hearing it and stated that it represented their own thoughts and feelings. Nothing that has happened before or since ever brought the satisfaction of that conversation.

John C. Mohawk

Preamble
Chief Oren Lyons

Arrival

"Why are you here?" a Swiss official of the customs and immigration asked. "Are you real red Indians?"

"From the storybooks?" I answered with a question. He was taken aback by the thought. He was uncertain and didn't reply. We looked at each other, both for the first time. He slowly nodded in agreement.

"Perhaps," he said. At that moment we both realized that this was going to be a long encounter.

Indeed we were "real." Our presence—with our bright colors, ribbons, long hair, and feathers—at once reinforced stereotypes. At the same time, he was not prepared for the intense and intelligent challenge in our eyes. That was the context of our arrival in Europe in 1977. It was obvious to each of us that there would be a lot to learn from both camps, and so began our journey.

How Did We Get There?

Deskaheh, a Cayuga chief from the Six Nation Territory in Ohsweken, Ontario, Canada, traveled to Geneva in 1923 to register a complaint before the League of Nations. His complaint was against Canada for unilateral interference and removal of the governing body of traditional chiefs of the Haudenosaunee. His mission was blocked by Great Britain, which was the protectorate, as Canada was within the British Empire. However, Deskaheh did raise the support of other nations, and the Labor Party sponsored a public hearing in Geneva that continues to resonate even now. Deskaheh forged the trail for Indigenous nations today.

Oren Lyons, Onondaga Chief, entering West Germany with Six Nations passport.

How we came to arrive in Geneva in 1977 is a long story. The stories of the many Indigenous delegations who journeyed to Geneva in 1977 are essentially the same, because our oppressors are the same and share the same institutions and purpose: to gain our lands and control their resources. We owe our survival to the political will and spiritual integrity of our grandfathers and grandmothers and Indigenous nations and peoples wherever they may be.

For the Indigenous peoples of the Western Hemisphere, the landfall of Christopher Columbus brought disease, chaos, and catastrophe. Our oppression has been relentless, fueled by the greed of our brothers from Europe for God, glory, and gold. Sitting Bull, a Lakota patriot and spiritual leader, said "They kept but one promise. They promised to take our lands and they took them." How did they accomplish this? Simply by declaration.

Columbus came armed with not only cannons but with the Inter Caetera Bulls of Pope Nichols V (Bulls *Dum Diversas*, 1452, and *Romanus Pontifex*, 1455) and Pope Alexander VI (1492 and *Inter Caetera*, 1493).

These Inter Caetera Bulls evolved quickly into a "doctrine of discovery" that became institutionalized into the Law of Nations.

Indigenous peoples native to North, Central, and South America were instantly disenfranchised by these racist declarations. We were stigmatized as "heathens," "pagans," and "barbarous infidels," uncivilized and incapable of rational thought. But above all, we were not Christians. Using these self-serving declarations, the European Christians moved rapidly to establish Christian dominion over the entire Western Hemisphere. Indigenous peoples were designated as part of the flora and fauna and granted only the right of occupancy in our own lands. Because of this great conspiracy, Indigenous peoples have not been considered equals in the world of humanity. The Law of Nations decreed that any lands "discovered" by a Christian nation first, secured the title. Other Christian nations must respect the right of "first discovery." Further, if no Christians were living there, the lands were declared "empty," *terra nullius*, open for the taking, regardless of Native populations inhabiting it.

The Law of Nations forever displaced Indigenous peoples in our own lands. The "doctrine of discovery" doomed us to centuries of merciless and tragic struggles that continue to the present. That's why we went to Geneva in 1977, and that's why states continue to refuse to recognize our **right to self-determination** today.

We came with the hope that we would find enlightened people with a sense of justice. Naively, we thought if people heard our truths that they would help correct these great injustices. We learned differently. We had exchanged one field of battle for another. We discovered that the conspiracy of 1492 continues today.

The five hundredth anniversary of the "discovery" of the Americas came and went, and the Roman Catholic Church adamantly refused to apologize to Indigenous peoples for the murders and suffering they caused in the name of God. I wonder if they at least apologized to God.

The Indigenous peoples of the Americas saw the United Nations as a beacon of fairness and justice. We had read the 1948 Universal Declaration of Human Rights, and we considered ourselves human beings with those rights. We put a lot of faith in the principles espoused by the United Nations. We had great hopes and high expectations. We believed that people of authority and influence would respond to the outrages visited upon our peoples over the centuries. We didn't see the differences between invitations from the international nongovernmental organizations (NGOs) and the member states of the United Nations. All we knew was that we were invited to the UN in Geneva to enter grievances and speak our minds. This news reverberated throughout Indian Country in the Americas. At last hope and the opportunity to speak on our own behalf. It was a historical moment, a watershed event that has affected millions of lives around the globe.

These events did not occur in a vacuum. The sixties and seventies were decades of action in Indian Country. Drugs were a part of the war in Vietnam and the "scene" in America. The war in Vietnam was in full swing, creating an energy among young people that was enormous in scope and intensity. Peace versus war; flower children versus the establishment; the Civil Rights Movement of black America; the assassinations of John F. Kennedy, Robert Kennedy, and Martin Luther King, Jr.; the Kent State massacre of students; and the ominous and ever-mounting body count of American soldiers in Vietnam. The contrary energies of the times produced hippies, great music, and counterculture heroes: Jack Kerouac, Timothy O'Leary, Ram Dass, Janis Joplin, Muhammad Ali, Wavy Gravy, Santana, Pete Seeger, Jane Fonda, Jimmy Hendrix, Ina May and Stephen Gaskin, Bob Dylan, The Grateful Dead, The Doors, The Beatles, and Indians!

Images of Indians were everywhere. Indians were "in." You saw them in many of the psychedelic posters of Bill Graham's Filmore West. Indians were the perfect icon for the idealistic innocence and free spirit of the times. Indians represented integrity, courage, honor, and peace, and still do for that matter. Long hair was a statement of the times. Youth was on the move. They followed the music. They marched in protests and gathered at concerts like Woodstock that would be markers in the social history of America. America was on the road, challenging the direction of the U.S. military policies in Vietnam and supporting the Civil Rights Movement of American minorities. In this process they found Indian Country. This was the Age of Aquarius.

At the same time, Indian Country was awash with actions and activities. The pan-Indian movement, based upon the return to the traditional values of Indian life, had morphed into the **Unity Caravan**. Iroquois and Hopi elders were the core of the campaign to reassert the importance of language; ceremony; and the values of community, service, and sharing back into our villages and nations. We challenged the hundred-year policies of the United States Bureau of Indian Affairs (BIA) and the Canadian Department of Indian Affairs (DIA), organized to destroy our languages, ceremonies, cultures, and spiritual centers. Despite these attacks—coupled with boarding schools, mission schools, and social engineering—our heathen and pagan instincts remained strong, and we clung to Mother Earth for survival. We still know who we are.

In Geneva: Larry Red Shirt, Lee Lyons, Oren Lyons, and Clan Mother Audrey Shenandoah.

Photograph courtesy Oren Lyons.

Traditional American Indian leaders became proactive. We gathered from Canada, Oklahoma, South Dakota, North Dakota, Montana, Arizona, California, Maine, Florida, New York, and Washington State. Our Unity Caravan circled the United States and parts of Canada four times from 1967 to 1971. The traditional leaders of that time were Thomas and Fermina Banyacya, David and Jack Monongye, and Mina Lansa, all from Hopi. Chief Leon Shenandoah, Cecelia and Chief Irving Powless, Sr., Audrey Shenandoah, and Chief Louie Farmer, all from Onondaga. Chief Beaman and Arlene Logan came from Seneca, Mad Bear Anderson from Tuscarora, Chief Mose David and Chief Louie Thompson from Mohawk. Henry Knockwood, Mi'Kmaq; Sam Sapio, Penobscot; Bill Cammanda, Algonquin; Buster McCurdy, Ute; Oscar Boland, Cherokee; Clifford Hill, Cherokee; Lame Deer, Lakota; Don McCloud and Janet McCloud, Puyallup and Tulalip; Al Bridges and

Edith McCloud, Puyallup and Tulalip. Then there were the runners. That's where I was most useful. We would get directions from the elders and carry them out. My brother Lee Lyons was in that category, and a younger group was also very active. Notable among that group were Tracy and Jeannie Shenandoah, brother and sister from Onondaga, and Tom Porter, Mohawk.

There were more, but those who are named were the principal activists in the development and implementation of the Unity Caravan. My life was very much affected by those years of action and activity.

The Indians of the Northwest Coast were embroiled in what is now known as the "fishing wars." In the sixties and seventies, the **American Indian Movement** (**AIM**) developed in St. Paul and Minneapolis, Minnesota, to counteract work exploitation, discrimination, and police brutality suffered by the large American Indian population in the twin cities. Russell Means, Oglala Lakota, and Dennis Banks, Anishinabe, were coleaders in the young activist movement that soon became a target for federal surveillance and harassment. AIM received requests for support from Indians under stress in Indian Country and urban centers in large cities across the country. The termination and relocation policies of the Eisenhower-Nixon administration were responsible for moving large American Indian populations off their native lands and territories into cities, causing great stress for the new arrivals and their neighbors.

In 1969, Richard Oaks, a young Mohawk ironworker, led the occupation of the abandoned prison on Alcatraz Island in San Francisco Bay. This celebrated occupation gained international attention and galvanized Indian Country in support. Native youth were demanding a return to their heritage.

In quick succession there was the occupation of the BIA building in Washington, DC, in 1972. Blunders by federal agencies resulted in the first occupation in Washington, DC, since the War of 1812, through no fault of the Indians. Four months later, AIM was invited to Pine Ridge, South Dakota, by the Oglala Sioux Civil Rights Organization and the traditional chiefs of the Oglala Sioux led by Chief Fools Crow. They wanted support of their fight to remove the Pine Ridge tribal chairman, Richard Wilson, who was accused of corruption and trading away Lakota land. This turned into a seventy-one-day occupation that caught the world's attention. The Lakota Treaty Council sent two representatives to the Onondaga Nation in New York to request support and advice. Larry Red Shirt and Louie Bad Wound gained that support, and in 1973 the Haudenosaunee and the Oglala Sioux made a Treaty of Peace and Mutual Support. The FBI, federal marshals, BIA tribal police, and local vigilantes had closed all access

Wounded Knee, 1973: This striking photograph from one of the negotiations between the independent Oglala Nation and the U.S. government is telling of the way the Indian reality is thrown out of focus by Western law. The Wounded Knee struggle of the early 1970s questioned the legality of the Indian Reorganization Act (IRA) used by the government to carry on a reign of terror on Oglala Nation territories. The IRA was fully backed by U.S. law—which further intensified the repression by tying up several hundred community people in court cases.

Delegates at the plenary session during the Geneva Conference raise fists clenched in unity. From left to right: Chief Oren Lyons, Iroquois Confederacy; Juan Aguilar, Peru; Antonio Millape, Mapuche Confederation, Chile; Clyde Bellecourt, Anishinabe-Ojibwe; Marie Sanchez, Cheyenne; Rose Charlie, Indian Homemakers Association of Canada. Seated in front: Phillip Deere, Muskogee; and David Spotted Horse, Lakota. Standing with raised fists: Bill Wapepah, Kickapoo; and Greg Zephier, Ihanktowan Nakota (Yankton Sioux).

to Wounded Knee to the national and international media. This caused a high moment of crisis for the defenders at Wounded Knee. Marlon Brando, who won an Oscar for playing Don Corleone in *The Godfather,* effectively broke that news blockade by sending Sasheen Little Feather to the Academy Awards in Hollywood in his place to refuse to accept the award because of the shameful behavior of United States forces at Wounded Knee. We experienced immediate relief as world attention was refocused back on Wounded Knee, South Dakota. The occupation ground to a bitter end that resulted in incarceration for some and the end of Richard Wilson's regime. These are just a few of the incidents that led up to the trip to Geneva in 1977.

The Decade of the Indigenous Peoples

There were and continue to be many reasons for Indigenous peoples to be present in the halls of the United Nations. For North American Indians and other Indigenous peoples with treaties, the UN provides a forum for discussion, studies, and possible solutions to protect Native lands and territories. The UN provides a forum to finally do away with the effects of the racist "doctrine of discovery" foisted upon generations of Native peoples and secure a brighter future for the 300 million or so Indigenous peoples of the world.

We have made great strides in the international forums on human rights over these past twenty-seven years. From the first discussion in 1970 by the UN Sub-Commission on the Prevention of Discrimination and Protection of Minorities on the rights of Indigenous populations and the appointment of José R. Martínez Cobo of Ecuador as Special Rapporteur of this study, to the opening of the third session of the Permanent Forum on Indigenous Issues (a subsidiary organ of the United Nations' Economic and Social Council, known as ECOSOC) in May 2004, there can be no doubt progress has been made.

Much has taken place in between: in the halls of the United Nations; in the lands and territories of Indigenous peoples; and in world conferences on populations, social development, women, habitat, and treaties. There have been recommendations for ways to recognize and honor the needs of Indigenous peoples. Yet the central issues remain unresolved.

Basic Call to Consciousness is essentially the report brought to Geneva in 1977 by the Haudenosaunee. Sotsisowah, John Mohawk, a Haudenosaunee scholar, was given the task of drafting our message to the world. The draft was presented to the Grand Council of the Chiefs and examined word by word. After many changes, refinements, additions, and deletions, the draft became our report to the world. Whatever the outcome of this conference would be, the Haudenosaunee Council of Chiefs were satisfied that our report was what we wanted to present at Geneva.

I was given the task to deliver the opening statement at the UN. We had discussed the importance of that message, and we decided to speak for the Natural World since they could not speak for themselves. Our message reflected our concern for the life of future generations. Their welfare is predicated on the health of the Earth. Our observation is that the message we delivered twenty-seven years ago fell upon the deaf ears of authority.

Yes, our human rights have moved, almost imperceptively, forward. Yes, the Working Group for Indigenous Populations (WGIP) was a major step forward when it was created in 1982. It provided the platform for the

Study on Treaties, Agreements, and Other Constructive Arrangements between States and Indigenous Populations by Special Rapporteur Professor Miguel Alfonso Martinez. This important study was commissioned in 1989 and completed in 1994. But you will note the treaties are between states and "populations," not peoples or nations. So the oppressive directives of the thirteenth century Papal Bulls live on.

During the early years of our travels to Geneva we became increasingly aware that not only were we not recognized as peoples, which precludes us from human rights, but we had little or no rights in the eyes of the world. We were politically invisible.

The Working Group on Indigenous Populations made it possible to begin the task of drafting our own declaration of our rights. This evolved, after years of work, into the *Draft Declaration on the Rights of the World's Indigenous Peoples*. The draft provides a benchmark of minimum standards for Native peoples around the world. The draft declaration was adopted by the Sub-Commission on Prevention of Discrimination and Protection of Minorities in 1993. The Commission on Human Rights is now reviewing the draft. This review is dragging on; currently they have accepted only two of the forty-five articles. The draft is stuck on Article 3, which addresses self-determination:

> Indigenous peoples have the right to self-determination and can freely determine their own political status and identity.

States, particularly the United States with support from Australia, have blocked the passage of this article at every session and have threatened to withdraw unless the wording is revised. So much for democracy.

The voices of Indigenous peoples were strong in Rio in 1992. At this United Nations' Earth Summit, which focused on Agenda 21, women, children, and Indigenous peoples were included for special concern. We fought hard to be included, but little came from it. As a matter of fact, in the ten year follow-up at the World Summit on Sustainable Development, Johannesburg, South Africa, we were virtually unmentioned in the final report. If it wasn't for a few Indigenous representatives, luckily still at the conference, lobbying hard at the last hour of the last day for our continued inclusion in the Convention on Biological Diversity, we would have been completely eliminated from any reference at all. So the conspiracy of 1492 and 1493 lives on.

In 1989 we began lobbying the United Nations to recognize 1992 as "The Year of the World's Indigenous People." This was to coincide with the 500th anniversary of the "discovery" of the Western Hemisphere by Columbus. We knew that countries were preparing big celebrations, including the reconstruction of the Santa Maria. Spain and Italy were foremost in these celebrations, with the United States and Central and South America scheduling similar events. We, the Indigenous peoples of the North, Central, and South Americas, were just as determined to challenge the myths and lies that passed for the history of this event.

Spain, Italy, and other member states of the United Nations defeated our efforts to have the initial recognition of Indigenous peoples fall on the anniversary of the so-called "discovery" of the Americas. However, we had generated so much pressure that the United Nations proclaimed 1993 as the "Year of the World's Indigenous People." Ultimately this worked out for us, because, by my calculations, Indigenous peoples defeated Columbus in the international field of public opinion in 1992, and our issues continued to roll on into 1993 with great momentum.

The following year the general assembly proclaimed 1995 to 2004 as the International Decade of the World's Indigenous People. Great. We'll take it, along with the observation that we are no longer "populations," we are now "people," not yet "peoples" with an "s," but that will come if we persevere. After all, we are peoples, are we not? In the full international sense of the word. And in the eyes of the Creator.

The mandates of the Decade of the World's Indigenous People have not been met, and by all assessments the decade is an abysmal failure. There seems to be no political will on the part of states to take positive action on these issues. It may take another decade for any of the mandates to be implemented.

Yet again a benchmark step was taken with the establishment of the Permanent Forum on Indigenous Issues as a subsidiary organ of ECOSOC in July 2000. Indigenous organizations may participate in the forum's work as observers. With the establishment of the Special Rapporteur on the Situation of the Human Rights and Fundamental Freedoms of Indigenous Peoples, there now is an avenue for Indigenous peoples to register complaints with the Division of Human Rights, an avenue that previously did not exist.

Still, this is a forum on Indigenous "issues" and not peoples. So we're here and not here. And the Inter Caetera Bulls of the Medieval Church of Rome continues to be the defining law for Indigenous peoples.

Throughout this outline of the international history of contemporary Native peoples there has been little or no discussion about nature, Mother Earth, and Natural Law, the ultimate authority regarding life on Earth. This is where "all the King's men" will not prevail.

Some time ago, perhaps sixteen or seventeen years back, Indian leaders were sitting around a campfire in Lakota Country. It was night and the stars were brilliant. A camp coffeepot was hot by the fire, and we were talking about our greedy brother from across the sea. It was the usual talk of what he was doing now to the Earth, to the people, and to himself. Louie Bad Wound stood up and cursed in disgust. He said, "You know what we should do? Look at how many medicine people are here. We should put our medicines together and call in the winds and storms. Flood 'em out! We should call in the fires and burn 'em out! Maybe then he'll listen."

We were surprised by Louie's outburst and we said, "Louie, maybe we ought to think that one over."

Louie answered and said, "Well, he's not going to listen any other way!"

We settled Louie down and talked about the damage being done to Mother Earth. I remember the sparks flying into the night and how we all grew silent thinking about Louie's words.

Louie has long gone to the "other side camp," but I think of his words often. Now I think if Louie were here he would see that that our greedy brother has brought the winds and fire himself. What Louie was asking for is here. Mother Earth is in the process of bringing balance back to herself, and we will begin to suffer the consequences. This is our opportunity to make him listen.

These elements will only increase in intensity, and it will be very democratic. We all live under the law of flesh, bone, and blood, and we are subject to that law. There is no place to run. Disease is on the move, outsmarting modern medicine. We're depleting the resources of the world. Water will fuel the next wars. Global warming is on the march and world leaders continue to ignore it.

Economies are so fragile that natural disasters will destroy national economies. We are so dependent on energy that we are helpless without it. Climate changes and weather patterns are now in flux, yet our leaders fight wars over oil, spending enormous sums of money for military arms that could be better spent for food, shelter, medicine, and education for our future generations.

We need to mobilize for peace with the same energy that we use to mobilize for war. We need to produce better leaders with values of community and sharing. We need to exercise common sense.

The Great Peacemaker came among our people a thousand years ago with a message of peace. He said people must have equity and good minds and health. He instructed our leaders on governance. He said, "When you sit in council for the welfare of the people, think not of yourself, your family, or even your generation. Make all of your decisions on behalf of the seventh generation coming, then you yourself will have peace."

We must look back and recognize those that sacrificed for us seven generations ago so that we may have what we have today. They set high moral standards and kept the laws that respected the Earth. We prosper today because of the work of those delegates and leaders who are no longer here. We must look forward and keep firm the standards they set for us, and continue to fight for the seventh generation coming. Our work represents peace for them. When they read and experience this *Declaration on the Rights of the World's Indigenous Peoples* and experience their right to self-determination, in the full sense of the word, equal to all under law, they will think kindly of us and sing songs about us, because they will know that we loved them.

Dhnayto. (Now I am finished.)

Joagquisho–Oren Lyons
Faithkeeper
Onondaga Nation
Haudenosaunee
Six Nations Iroquois Confederacy

The Haudenosaunee
A Nation
Since Time Immemorial

The Haudenosaunee, more commonly known as the Iroquois Confederacy, are an ancient people of North America. Our tradition states that our people originated in the northeastern woodlands of North America. There are no stories within that tradition concerning migration across frozen lands to the area we occupy. We have been and continue to be the original inhabitants of these lands.

Our existence in these lands has not been one of absolute peace and tranquility. We have had to work hard to develop the civilization we enjoy. There was a time when our lands were torn by conflict and death. There were times when certain individuals attempted to establish themselves as the rulers of the people through exploitation and repression.

We emerged from those times to establish a strong democratic and spiritual Way of Life. The confederate state of the Haudenosaunee became the embodiment of democratic principles that continue to guide our peoples today. The Haudenosaunee became the first "United Nations," established on a firm foundation of peace, harmony, and respect.

Within the Haudenosaunee, all member nations are equal, regardless of size. Within their national territories the member nations are autonomous, but all adhere to the central principles of democracy that we agreed to at the formation of the Confederacy.

The national Councils of Chiefs do not govern the people; instead they act as representatives of their clans in a process that coordinates the wishes of the people. They also act as judiciary in serious disputes that people cannot resolve among themselves.

The confederated Council of Chiefs, or Grand Council, acts as the coordinating body of the will and determination of the member nations. The Grand Council also has the responsibility of conducting affairs with other states and nations.

All of this political activity is set in the roots of an ancient tradition of the spirituality of our peoples. This cosmology places the Haudenosaunee in a balanced, familiar relationship with the universe and the Earth. In our languages, the Earth is our Mother Earth, the sun our Eldest Brother, the moon our Grandmother, and so on. It is the belief of our people that all elements of the Natural World were created for the benefit of all living things and that we, as humans, are one of the weakest of the whole Creation, since we are totally dependent on the whole Creation for our survival.

This philosophy taught us to treat the Natural World with great care. Our institutions, practices, and technologies were developed with a careful eye to their potential for disturbing the delicate balance in which we lived.

European peoples first made contact with Haudenosaunee peoples early during the seventeenth century. The Dutch occupation of the Hudson River, and the English colonies on the Connecticut River and in Rhode Island, resulted in conflicts that rapidly escalated to warfare and that resulted in the massacre of the Algonkian-speaking peoples in those areas.

The European invasion of the North American Continent brought radical and permanent changes in the nature and objectives of warfare. The very first contact between Europeans and the people of the Haudenosaunee resulted in the deaths of a number of Mohawk people at the hands of a contingent under the command of Samuel de Champlain.

Within three decades our people were embroiled in a life-and-death struggle that was triggered by conflicts between two imperialist powers over trade in furs and agricultural settler colonies.

During this period of colonial warfare, our country received a massive influx of refugees fleeing from the invaders. At the same time, our lands were invaded on several occasions by European armies that carried out "burnt earth" policies against our people with an intensity that had never been seen in our part of the world. The Haudenosaunee survived those attacks, and we consummated numerous international treaties of peace and friendship with Holland, England, and France.

By the time of the American Revolution, the people of the Haudenosaunee had experienced over one hundred fifty years of intermittent warfare. The conclusion of the revolution brought into existence the world's first settler state, and our struggle for survival entered a new phase.

In 1784, our government negotiated a treaty of peace and friendship with the newly formed United States.[1] Almost immediately, we were faced with the establishment of illegal American settlements within the lands defined in the treaty. Scattered skirmishes and conflicts were occurring throughout our lands.

At about this time, the state of New York was attempting to negotiate its own treaties with our peoples. The settlers knew that our governing councils would never relinquish lands or allow their settlements. In response, New York began the practice of negotiating with any Native person who might grant them the concessions, especially the land concessions, they wished. Dozens of state treaties were signed by people who were under the influence of alcohol at the time and who often represented no one. A number of treaties were made that bear signatures that are outright forgeries.[2]

All of this was occurring at a time when the years of warfare and disease had taken a heavy toll within our communities. The spirit of many people had been broken, and they had taken to drinking or had sunk into states of apathy. All of this was to the advantage of unscrupulous settlers.

From 1784 to 1838, most of the Haudenosaunee territory was taken under fraudulent treaty or treaties obtained through coercion.[3] Many of our people fled to lands promised them by the British Crown, lands that are now within the area shown on European maps as Canada. A number of our people were coerced, cajoled, and otherwise forced to relocate to lands in Oklahoma, Kansas, and Wisconsin.

It was during this time that a chief of the Confederacy named Handsome Lake began to articulate a vision of liberation and resistance. His words became the guiding force that saved our peoples from complete cultural destruction during a period when Native culture was on the brink of annihilation throughout northeastern North America. His teachings continue to act as a guide for our people in the work we must carry on to ensure our survival as a distinct people of the world. His vision made clear the nature of the enemy, for he explained the way in which the colonizers would use their institutions and laws, not only to gain our lands, but also our minds and our self-esteem.

Throughout the 1800s and 1900s, every aspect of this vision has proven true. The initial assaults against our culture were carried out by missionaries and "educators." The historical record provides ample proof that there was a deliberate and concerted effort during this period to destroy our laws, customs, spiritual beliefs, and languages.

The ultimate purpose of that strategy became clear as both the United States and the Canadian governments passed laws and adopted policies that were intended to assimilate our people and our remaining territories into those countries.

In 1892, New York State forcibly placed an illegal government in the Mohawk territory of Akwesasne[4] and passed laws restricting the traditional governments in our territories. Canada acted with the same strategy at about the same time.[5]

In 1923, one of our leaders, a Cayuga chief named Deskaheh, attempted to take our complaints to the League of Nations in Geneva, Switzerland. He was unsuccessful, although he did receive the support of many sympathetic Swiss people. He died in exile when the Canadian government refused to allow him to return to his homeland.

The next year the United States passed citizenship laws that ostensibly imposed citizenship upon Indigenous peoples.[6] The Haudenosaunee notified both the U.S. and Canada[7] that we would not accept citizenship and that we would remain citizens of our own country. Canada responded by sending a military contingent to the Grand River Country and erecting a military barracks there, occupying the territory and forcibly expelling the traditional government.[8]

In 1934, the United States passed the Indian Reorganization Act (IRA),[9] which was designed to destroy the traditional governments and to place Native peoples under the supervision of the secretary of the Department of the Interior.

In two separate bills passed in 1948 and 1950, the United States Congress granted New York State civil and criminal jurisdiction over the Haudenosaunee territories.[10]

During the early 1950s, the Haudenosaunee lost thousands of acres of land to dams, water reservoirs, highways, electrical and gas lines, and the St. Lawrence Seaway.[11]

None of these events has occurred without resistance from our peoples. In all of our territories there have been confrontations with police forces. There have been many attempts to stop these attacks against our land base, and many court battles have been fought.

During the 1970s, a new strategy began to unfold for the Haudenosaunee. In the Onondaga territory, New York State was stopped from expanding an interstate highway.[12] The international bridge that passes through Akwesasne was blockaded until unrestricted passage for our people was obtained. In 1974, our people undertook the reoccupation of part of our homeland that had been illegally taken by the United States.[13]

Throughout that time, several other Haudenosaunee communities underwent a revitalization of community culture with a strong emphasis on our economic, educational, and spiritual Way of Life. Between 1979 and 1981, the Mohawk Nation at Akwesasne gained international attention as the struggle against the colonial government imposed by the United States, involving hundreds of community residents, intensified.

We have consistently been aggressive in asserting that we are a state, a government, and a people who have a right to a place in the international community. In 1977, we sent a twenty-one person delegation to take part in the International Non-Governmental Organization's conference on "Discrimination Against the Indigenous Populations of the Americas," held in Geneva, Switzerland.[14] All twenty-one people traveled on passports issued by our government and have since visited a number of other countries with these passports.

The position papers we presented at that conference are in this book and serve to underline our position. As the 1980s began, we were a people confident about our future and clear about the nature of our struggle.

Segwalise

Thoughts of Peace: The Great Law

Haudenosaunee oral history related that long before the Europeans arrived, Native peoples of the northeast woodlands had reached a crisis. It is said that during this time, a man or woman might be killed or injured by his or her enemies for any slight offense, and that blood feuds between clans and villages ravaged the people until no one was safe. It was during this time that a male child was born to a woman of the Wyandot people living on the north side of Lake Ontario near the Bay of Quinte. It would become the custom of the people of the Longhouse that this person's name would never be spoken except during the recounting of this oral history in the oral fashion (some say it during the Condolence Ceremony). At other times he is addressed simply as "the Peacemaker."

The Peacemaker became one of the great political philosophers and organizers in human history. It is impossible in this short essay to discuss more than a brief outline of his ideas and accomplishments, but it should become obvious that his vision for humankind was indeed extraordinary.

He concluded early in life that the system of blood feuds, as practiced by the people inhabiting the forest at that time, needed to be abolished. His ideas were rejected by the Wyandot and other Huron peoples and while a young man, he journeyed to the land of the People of the Flint located on the southeast shore of Lake Ontario and extending to the areas called today the Mohawk Valley. The People of the Flint, or Kanien'kehá:ka, are known to English-speaking peoples as the Mohawks.

Upon arrival in the Mohawk Country, he began seeking out those individuals who had the reputation as being the fiercest and most fearsome destroyers of human beings. He sought them out one at a time—murderers and hunters of humans, even cannibals—and he brought to each one his message.

The first Grand Council with Peacemaker
holding a white wampum belt.

One by one he "straightened out their minds" as each grasped the
principles that he set forth. Nine men of the Mohawks—the nine most
feared men in all Mohawk Country—grasped hold of his words and
became his disciples.

The first principle that the Peacemaker set forth was indisputable to
those who heard his words. He said that it has come to pass that in this
land human beings are seen to abuse one another. He pointed to the world
in which people live and said that people should consider that some force
or some thing must have created this world—the Giver of Life—that had not
intended that human beings would abuse one another. Human beings
whose minds are healthy always desire peace, and humans have minds that
enable them to achieve peaceful resolutions of their conflicts.

From that initial explanation—that the Giver of Life (later addressed as
the Great Creator) did not intend that human beings abuse one another—
he proposed that human societies must form governments that will serve to
prevent the abuse of human beings by other human beings and that will
ensure peace among nations and peoples. Government would be established for the purpose of abolishing war and robbery among brothers and
to establish peace and quietness. He drew the Mohawks together under
those principles and then went to the Oneidas, Onondagas, Cayugas, and
Senecas with the same teachings. What is unique about his work is that he

not only set forth the argument that government is desirable, he also set forth the principle that government is specifically organized to prevent the abuse of human beings by cultivating a spiritually healthy society and the establishment of peace.

Other political philosophers and organizers have come to the conclusion that governments can be formed for the purpose of establishing tranquility, but the Peacemaker went considerably further than that. He argued not for the establishment of law and order, but for the full establishment of peace. Peace was to be defined not as the simple absence of war or strife, but as the active striving of humans for the purpose of establishing universal justice. Peace was defined as the product of a society that strives to establish concepts that correlate to the English words power, reason, and righteousness.

"Righteousness" refers to something akin to the shared ideology of the people using their purest and most unselfish minds. It occurs when the people put their minds and emotions in harmony with the flow of the universe and the intentions of the "Good Mind" or the Great Creator. The principles of righteousness demand that all thoughts of prejudice, privilege, or superiority be swept away, and that recognition be given to the reality that the creation is intended for the benefit of all equally—even the birds, animals, trees, and insects, as well as the humans. The world does not belong to humans—it is the rightful property of the Great Creator. The gifts and benefits of the world, therefore, belong to all equally. The things that humans need for survival—food, clothing, shelter, protection—are things to which all are entitled because they are gifts of the Great Creator. Nothing belongs to human beings, not even their labor or their skills, for ambition and ability are also the gifts of the Great Creator.

Therefore all people have a right to the things they need for survival, even those who do not or cannot work, and no person or people has a right to deprive others of the fruits of those gifts.

"Reason" is perceived to be the power of the human mind to make righteous decisions about complicated issues. The Peacemaker began his teachings based on the principle that human beings were given the gift of the power of reason in order that they may settle their differences without the use of force. He proposed that in every instance humans should use every effort to counsel about, arbitrate, and negotiate their differences, and that force should be resorted to only as a defense against the certain use of force. All men whose minds are healthy can desire peace, he taught, and there is an ability within all human beings, and especially in the young human beings, to grasp and hold strongly to the principles of righteousness.

The ability to grasp the principles of righteousness is a spark within the individual that society must fan and nurture so that it may grow. Reason is seen as the skill that humans must be encouraged to acquire in order that the objectives of justice may be attained and no one's rights abused.

Having established the concept of righteousness and reason, the Peacemaker went on to discuss the nature of "power." The power to enact a true peace is the product of a unified people on the path of righteousness, and reason is the ability to enact the principles of peace through education, public opinion, and political, and when necessary, military unity. The "power" that the Peacemaker spoke of was intended to enable the followers of the law to call upon warring or quarreling parties to lay down their arms and to begin a peaceful settlement of their disputes. Peace, as the Peacemaker understood it, flourished only in a garden amply fertilized with absolute and pure justice. It was the product of a spiritually conscious society using its abilities of reason that resulted in a healthy society. The power to enact peace (which requires that people cease abusing one another) was conceived to be both spiritual and political.

But it was power in all the senses of the word—the power of persuasion and reason, the power of the inherent goodwill of humans, the power of a dedicated and united people, and, when all else failed, the power of force.

The principles of law set forth by the Peacemaker sought to establish a peaceful society by eliminating the causes of conflict between individuals and between peoples. It was a law that was conceived prior to the appearance of classes, and it sought to anticipate and eliminate anything that took the appearance of group or class interest, even in the form of clan or tribal interest, especially in the area of property. The law was also based to an impressive degree on a logic that looked to nature for its rules. It is one of the few examples of a "Natural Law" that is available to modern man. It is a law that clearly precedes "royal law," or "mercantile law," or "bourgeois property-interest law."

The government that is established under the Great Law provides, in effect, that the leaders or "chiefs" are the servants of the people. Everyone in the Six Nations, wherever the law prevails, has direct participation in the workings of the government. Direct democracy, when it involves tens of thousands of people, is a very complex business, and there are many rules about how meetings are conducted. But the primary rule about the flow of power and authority is clearly that the power and authority of the people lies with the people and is transmitted by them through the "chiefs." The fact that all the people have direct participation in the decision of their governments is the key factor for the success and longevity of the Haudenosaunee.

Internally, the law was to be the power by which the people were united ideologically and administratively under a dispute settlement process to which all had agreed to submit and to remove those customs of the past that had sparked conflict and fostered disunity. The path to unity was a difficult one indeed. The territory of the People of the Longhouse had been composed of five distinct countries, and each sometimes jealously guarded their hunting lands from intrusion by the others. The Peacemaker abolished the concept of separate territories. The law unified the peoples, saying that they were distinct from one another only because they spoke different languages. He said the territories were common to all and that each individual member of any of the nations had full rights of hunting and occupation of all the lands of all the nations of the People of the Longhouse.

In terms of the internal affairs of the People of the Longhouse, the first and most important principle was that under the law the people of the nations were one people. Since the Haudenosaunee call themselves the People of the Longhouse, the Peacemaker's admonition was that under the law the country of the Haudenosaunee was itself a Longhouse, with the sky as its roof and the earth as its floor.

The peoples were assigned to clans by the Peacemaker, and so strong was to be the feeling of unity and oneness between them that the members of the clan of one nation were admonished not to marry members of the same clan of another nation, so closely were they now related. The law bound them together as blood relatives.

In one motion he abolished exclusive national territories and the concept of national minorities. Any member of the Five Nations was to have full rights in the country of any of the Five Nations with only one restriction—he or she did not have the right to hold high public office, though that right could be conferred upon them by the host nation if they so wished.

The idea that the nations were united as one meant that the nations who were members of the Confederacy had agreed to surrender a part of their sovereignty to the other nations of the Confederacy. The Confederacy Council was to be the forum under which foreign nations and peoples could approach the People of the Longhouse. Any decision concerning the disposition of Seneca lands must first pass through the Confederacy Council where the other nations, who also have rights in Seneca lands, can participate in the decision-making process.

The Peacemaker envisioned that the principles under which the Five Nations were governed could be extended far beyond the borders of the

The Great Tree of Peace.

Haudenosaunee to all the peoples of the world. The law of the Peacemaker provides that any nation or people may find protection under the Great Tree of Peace, which symbolized the laws of the Confederacy. He expected that the principles of the Confederacy would be well received by many nations, and that the Haudenosaunee would venture forth with the offer of a union that would be designed to prevent hostilities and lay the basis of peaceful coexistence. With that in mind, the Constitution of the Five Nations provides that any nation may seek its protection through becoming knowledgeable about the laws and agreeing to follow the principles set forth in it. Many Native nations accepted that offer.

The Five Nations agreed among themselves that in the event of an attack they would organize a military force to repel the invader and carry on the war in the invader's country until the war was concluded. The opponent had an absolute right to a cessation of the hostilities at any time by simply calling for a truce. At that point the process of negotiation went into action. The Constitution of the Five Nations prescribes that in the event another people are conquered, the Five Nations shall not impose upon them the Five Nations' religion, nor collect tribute from them, nor subject them to any form of injustice. The Five Nations would not seize their territory. What was demanded was that the offending nation of people put away their weapons of war and that they cease military aggression.

Any individual or group of individuals had the right, according to the Constitution, to approach the Five Nations, learn the law, and agree to abide by it. When that happened, they were to be offered the protection of the law and the People of the Longhouse.

The vision of the Peacemaker that all the peoples of the world would live in peace under the protection of a law that required that hostilities be outlawed and disputes offered a settlement process is yet today an exciting prospect. When the idea of a United Nations of the world was proposed toward the end of World War II, researchers were dispatched to find models in history for such an organization. For all practical purposes, the only model they found concerned the Constitution of the Five Nations, whose author had envisioned exactly that.

In a way, the Peacemaker was centuries ahead of his time. He set forth a system of government organization that was a marvelously complex enactment of the concept of participatory (as opposed to representative) democracy.

Under the rules of the law, councils of women appointed men who were to act more as conduits of the will of the people than as independent representatives of the people. The society was founded on concepts of moral justice, not statute law, and the rules of the society were designed to ensure that each member's rights were absolutely protected under the law. Women not only have rights but power as a community of people composing half of the population. The power of women has never been fully articulated by Western observers and interpreters of Haudenosaunee culture.

Peoples were recognized to have a right to exist unmolested as peoples in the articles of the Constitution. Individuals were recognized as having the full right to protection under the laws of the Confederacy—even individuals who were not members of the host nation—as long as they observed the rules of nonaggression and they didn't try to create factionalism among the people. The principle was set forth (and machinery to enact it was created) that provided that all peoples have a right to occupy their lands peacefully and that no one may deny them that right. A society was socialized to the ideology that, if an injustice occurs, it is their moral duty to defend the oppressed against their oppressors. The principle was set forth that no one has a right to deprive another of the fruits of his own labor, and that no one has a right to a greater share of the wealth of society than anyone else. The Peacemaker believed that if absolute justice was established in the world, peace would naturally follow.

Some of those ideas have begun to take root in the form of United Nations' statements and declarations made in recent years. The genius of the Peacemaker was that he not only set forth the principles, he also designed the machinery to enforce those principles. He seems to have operated on the assumption that universal justice is the product of a spiritually strong society, and many of the rules that he proposed are designed to create a strong society rather than a strong government. That is one of the ideas that has not been widely accepted in the twentieth century and certainly not in a context that the Peacemaker would have understood.

The Peacemaker set out to give some order to society and to create peace among peoples and nations. The rules that he set down were called by the Mohawks the "Great Goodness," and by the Senecas the "Great Law." The English called that body of teachings the "Constitution of the Five Nations." It has never been written down in English, despite allegations to the contrary by anthropologists. The versions that exist in English are highly inadequate efforts compared to the oral versions of the Great Law. This effort is no better—it does not compare in any way to the complexity, beauty, and eloquence of the Law.

Some people who have read the history of the Haudenosaunee will be able to point to episodes in the seventeenth and eighteenth centuries when some of the principles of this law appear to have been ignored. It is true that over nearly two centuries of intermittent warfare—warfare caused by pressures created by the expanding interests of European imperial nations—there was a considerable amount of social change and stress. French imperialist missionaries introduced the idea—an entirely foreign idea—that a divine will might guide the fortunes of people in government and in warfare. That kind of thinking was not to be found in the philosophies of the Peacemaker, but throughout history it has been an idea that has accompanied empire builders everywhere. Many ideas of European origin were adopted by different peoples of the Haudenosaunee at different times, ideas that were in conflict with the principles of the Great Law. In the almost two centuries since the beginning of the so-called "reservation" period, many more ideas that are in conflict with the principles of the Great Law have been imposed by the colonizers.

Most of what passes as "Iroquois history" was an effort by English and French historians to discredit the Haudenosaunee and to justify the destruction of the Confederacy and the theft of Confederacy lands. There were few instances when officials of the Confederacy violated the laws of the Great Peace, although individuals in any society do violate its laws. Following the American Revolution, the United States, and especially New York State, did everything in its power to dissolve the Confederacy and to deal with the individual nations. Great Britain, Canada, Ontario, and Québec have done

39

the same thing. Since the invasion of the Europeans, the Haudenosaunee have produced a number of patriots but few great philosophers. The outstanding Haudenosaunee philosopher and teacher of the post-contact period was also a Confederacy chief. His name was Handsome Lake, and he led a spiritual revitalization that produced an oral document called "The Good Word," a teaching on the same level of significance and power in Haudenosaunee culture as the Great Law. Combined, the two are a powerful teaching. Against incredible odds, the Confederacy has survived and has continued to this day. Its chiefs continue to meet periodically at the capital at Onondaga, and they continue to carry the titles bestowed upon them by the Peacemaker long before written history began. The ideas of the Confederacy continue to live also, and little by little the world is being exposed to those ideas. As long as those ideas remain alive, the possibility remains that the Peacemaker's vision of a world in peace and harmony may yet be realized.

Sotsisowah

Deskaheh: an Iroquois Patriot's Fight for International Recognition[1]

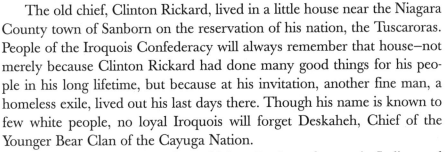

The old chief, Clinton Rickard, lived in a little house near the Niagara County town of Sanborn on the reservation of his nation, the Tuscaroras. People of the Iroquois Confederacy will always remember that house—not merely because Clinton Rickard had done many good things for his people in his long lifetime, but because at his invitation, another fine man, a homeless exile, lived out his last days there. Though his name is known to few white people, no loyal Iroquois will forget Deskaheh, Chief of the Younger Bear Clan of the Cayuga Nation.

Deskaheh was a descendent of Mary Jemison, famous in Indian and colonial history, and he was born in Grand River Land, a reservation of the Six Nations People who fled or were driven to British lands, now Canada, from their lands below the border after the American Revolution. They chose these acres, gratefully guaranteed to them by the British through General Haldimand,[2] because the Grand River, with its level flats, reminded them of their beloved lands taken over by New York State.

After his years of grammar school, Deskaheh, like many other Grand River people, exercised his rights, guaranteed by the Jay Treaty,[3] to cross the U.S. boundary to become a lumberjack in the Allegheny Mountains, but after an accident, he returned to Grand River and took up farming. He married the daughter of a Cayuga mother and white father, and she bore him four daughters and five sons.

By 1914, Deskaheh had reached the middle period of what white neighbors called a "successful reservation-Indian life." His honesty, sincerity, and ability as an orator in Cayuga language had brought him the deserved appointment as head speaker when the Canadian government, satisfied until the beginning of World War I to allow the Iroquois the status of a separate nation, decided on grounds of expediency to disregard the old treaties and assimilate the Indians, by force, if necessary. Deskaheh was the leader of the delegation that patiently explained in Ottawa, first, that the Canadian government had no jurisdiction over the little Iroquois nation, and second, that since the Indians had already volunteered in proportionately greater numbers than the people of any other nation in the world, an enforced draft of its young men by a foreign ally would seem silly.[4]

Deskaheh in Geneva, 1923.
Photo courtesy Tehanetorens (Ray Fadden), Six Nations Museum.

They won this argument, but the end of the war brought other attempted encroachment. The Iroquois soon knew that the majority in the legislative halls of the Canadian capitol planned further inroads on their rights as citizens of the separate country known as Grand River Land. In 1921, to thwart the purposes of these schemers, Deskaheh, appointed "Speaker of the Six Nations Council," presented as travel credentials a passport authorized by his nation and crossed the Atlantic to seek British aid.[5] Since, as he pointed out, the treaty by which his people had their rights guaranteed[6] was signed by George III, he asked for its confirmation by George V. The English authorities refused his request, saying that they would not deal with a Canadian domestic problem, and the Cayuga returned, disillusioned. Then the Canadian enemies grew bolder. Creating of a fifth-column party through persuasion, promises, and payments was easy. It was easier still to get the new minority to ask for protection. And it was easiest of all to order a detail of the red-jacketed Royal Canadian Mounted Police to ride into the Grand River country to

During the Geneva meetings in 1977, a Haudenosaunee chiefs' delegation was received by the Mayor of Geneva, who spoke about the Iroquois patriot, Deskaheh—well-remembered by the Swiss.

protect the "loyalist" Indians and "to keep the peace." So obvious was this procedure that Deskaheh, who strongly opposed it and pleaded earnestly for arbitration, won many sympathizers among his neighbors, and through them, news of the coming raid reached him in time for a hasty flight across the border of the United States to the city of Rochester in western New York State.

The raiders arrested and jailed a number of Iroquois, and though Deskaheh was known to abstain from alcohol, they searched his house on the pretext of looking for illegal beverages. The Canadian government then ordered barracks built for the housing of their police, and Grand River was suddenly an occupied nation.[7] Deskaheh now began to fight back desperately.

With the Six Nations' counsel, George P. Decker (a white, Rochester lawyer), as his companion, he again used his passport, this time to travel to Geneva to bring his peoples' case before the League of Nations.[8] He arrived in September 1923, took lodging in the Hotel des Families, and began to work toward personally presenting to the Council of the League the petition of his people. Though he met with no success, he fought doggedly. Winter came and went, and in mid-April he wrote to his wife and his sons and daughters, "I have no time to go anywhere, only sitting on the chair from morning till night, copying and answering letters as they come, and copying the documents, and I have many things to do." May came to the city by beautiful Lake Leman, but his thoughts were with his people beside the Grand River, and like a good believer in the religion of the Longhouse, he was seeking aid through the prayer of his people to their God. To his brother Alex General, he wrote: "I believe it will be a good thing to have a meeting in one of the Longhouses, but you must [combine] all the good people and the children of the Longhouse, only those that are faithful believers in our religion and no other, and it must be very early in the morning to have this, so that our God may hear you and the children, and ask him to help us in our distress at this moment, and you must use Indian tobacco in our usual way when we ask help to our Great Spirit . . . and you must have a uniform on . . . and also ask God you wish the religion will keep up for a great many years to come and the Indian race also. . . ."

By June he had obtained the services of a Swiss lawyer who was preparing a statement of the case of the Six Nations in French. The money the Indians and their friends had raised in North America was almost gone, and some means of replenishing it was necessary.

Again he wrote from Geneva to his brother Alex: "And we had a meeting of the Iroquois of the Six Nations of the Grand River Land [really the committee devoted to the interests of the Six Nations] on the 27th of June, and the meeting decided to raffle off the two portrait pictures which they made and just think of it, these two pictures of myself with my costume on brought six thousand Swiss francs—it means a little over one thousand dollars of our money, and it gives me very great lift to our fight . . . very strong committee, all big people, of high class people. When the meeting takes place everybody looks decent of their suit and dress very well." If these informal reports written to his beloved family in unfamiliar language seem naive, the campaign Deskaheh and his good friend, George Decker, were waging was not. It was hard-hitting, simple, direct.[9] The embarrassed officials who had to deny this representative of a small nation the right to speak before the League Council committed to the Wilsonian doctrine of autonomy for small nations. These two made the situation more awkward for the British interests by making public the prints distributed in Geneva, quotations from treaties, and documents that Canada had decided to abrogate as "scraps of paper."

The Cayuga chief was also attracting much favorable attention as a person. To the Irish woman correspondent of the *Freeman's Journal,* he

44

seemed a "good-looking, broad-shouldered man, about forty years of age [he was actually fifty-four] wearing ordinary dark clothes . . . and presenting every appearance of a well-to-do farmer with the one exception of his beautiful moccasins. . . ." She commented on the penetrating, searching glance of his dark eyes, his kindly smile disclosing remarkably white teeth, and finished her description with the sentence, "His beautifully shaped but stern mouth, firm chin, and heavy jawbones are those of the born fighter, the strong man who knows his strength and believes in it, whilst his shining eyes speak of enthusiasm and idealism." But in the middle of this enthusiastic and sentimental interview, the chief had persuaded her to quote from the text of a memorial address to the Grand River Indians, dated as late as December 4, 1912, and filed by Great Britain:

> The Documents, Records, and Treaties between the British Governors in former times, and your wise Forefathers, of which, in consequence of your request, authentic copies are now transmitted to you, all establish the Freedom and Independency of your Nations.

Time wore on, and though a few Englishmen and Canadians spoke up for the Six Nations Indians, though the representatives of the Netherlands and Albania listened sympathetically and spoke of supporting his petition, Deskaheh began to suspect that his cause was lost. News from the homeland was bad. The Canadian Government had announced a "free election," which would in effect determine whether or not the Six Nations Government of Grand River Land should be dissolved. For this vote, the Canadian Government agent had taken possession of the Six Nations Council House, surrounding it with a guard of twenty police. In protest the Indians favoring their nation's continuance did not vote.[10] The Canadian authorities then broke open the safe holding the records of the Six Nations and took from there a number of wampum belts, revered as sacred by the Iroquois, refusing, on demand, to return them. In November 1924, Deskaheh wrote to the editor of a Swiss journal,

> It is the heart broken that I must affirm that since several months I am against the most cruel indifference. . . . My appeal to the Society of Nations has not been heard, and nothing in the attitude of Governments does not leave me any hope.

> It is in this dreadful agony that I take the advantage to cry out that injustice, by the means of your free review, to my Brothers from all races and all religions. Too long we have suffered from the tyranny of our neighbors who tread under feet our Right and laugh at the Pact which binds them. . . . Our appeal is for all those

which are animated by the spirit of justice and we ask them their benevolent help.

As if to seal its own lack of interest, the Secretariat of the League that had notified Deskaheh of the refusal to allow him to appear as a petitioner before a plenary session, aware of the embarrassment he had caused, now denied both Deskaheh and George Decker seats in the gallery to observe deliberations.

Despairing, the two friends struck their last brave blow. They hired the *Salle Centrale*, and advertised in the press their own meeting at which Deskaheh would present the case of his nation to those who would come to listen. The response was amazing. The North American "Indian" had been a popular figure in Europe since the time of Columbus, and the populace, the vast majority of whom had never seen an example of the "noble savage" as popularized by translations from the works of James Fenimore Cooper and other romanticists, attended in thousands. All the Geneva Boy Scouts were present, but not a single League of Nation Official. Members of the press of many nations, sensing possibilities of stories about a picturesque if not politically important character, were at their reserved tables, among them the distinguished Hungarian journalist Aloys Derso, who told amusing and movingly pathetic incidents of the occasion.

> I went to the evening to see my first American Indian. He was in the dressing room already in full regalia. I drew a few sketches of him and he was a good model, sitting immobile. He had not the typical Indian profile, the nose not the aquiline nose I had expected. His eyes were tired and there was a great melancholy in his expression.

When Deskaheh appeared before the great audience, he walked in dignity and with no self-consciousness. There were giggles because, though he wore the elaborate dress of a Chief of the Cayuga Nation, he carried an enormous yellow suitcase that he placed carefully on a table in front of him.

Smiles soon ceased, however, as Deskaheh related his story simply and sincerely. His people had heard in 1915, he said, of a repulsively homely white chief of the British people. The young Indian men had swiftly formed a regiment and gone across the big water to fight for world freedom and justice as the allies of the government that had once so gratefully guaranteed his nation its lands. Here he repeated a passage from the Treaty of 1784,[11] as worded by Sir Frederick Haldimand, governor-in-chief of Québec and territories depending hereon:

I do hereby in His Majesty's name, authorize and permit the said Mohawk Nation and such others of the Six Nations Indians as wish to settle in that quarter to take possession of and settle upon the banks of the river commonly called Ouse or Grand River . . . which them and their posterity are to enjoy forever.

Then he recited the tale of the broken pledge, the raid of the Royal Mounted Police, the rummaging of his own house, the building of the police barracks, and the seizure of the sacred wampum. The story would be incredible without evidence, he said, but he had foreseen this and had the proofs with him. Then he lifted the lid of the suitcase and with care and reverence drew from within the old beaded wampum on which might be read the sworn agreements of white governments with his people. Speaking with deep feeling, translating these documents slowly and impressively, stopping now and then to make clear the meanings of the bead colors and of the representations of the symbols, he made his entranced listeners feel that this was not the narration of the grievances of a small racial unit, but the story of all minority peoples—the tragedy of every small nation that is a neighbor to a large one. When he finished, there was a moment of silence—then the roar of a tremendous ovation. Thousands rose to their feet to cheer him, and the great hall echoed and re-echoed with their applause. Straight, unsmiling, impassive, he waited until after many minutes the sound began to wane. Then, still expressionless, he left the platform.

Before the end of 1924, the Speaker of the Six Nations Council had returned to the United States, a disillusioned and discouraged man. An exile from Canada and from the nation he thought he had failed, he found refuge with Clinton Rickard in the house of the benign old chief.[12] There, by the Niagara River, which marks the Canadian boundary, he found that the people for whom he had fought did not think him a failure. From their northern homes in Grand River Land, they journeyed here to see him and assure him of their loyalty. Though his disheartening experience had weakened him physically, his spirit took fire from their words and, with never-ending courage, he kept up his battle.

The Last Speech of Deskaheh

On the evening of March 10, 1925, suffering from a serious attack of pleurisy and pneumonia, Deskaheh made his last speech. It was before a radio microphone in Rochester. Once more, and more forcefully than ever, he hurled defiance at big nations who disregard the claims of smaller peoples.[13]

Nearly everyone who is listening to me is a pale face, I suppose. I am not. My skin is not red, but that is what my people are called by others. My skin is brown, light brown, but our cheeks have a little flush and that is why we are called red skins. We don't mind that. There is no difference between us, under the skins, that any expert with a carving knife has ever discovered.

My home is on the Grand River. Until we sold off a large part, our country extended down to Lake Erie, where, one hundred forty winters ago, we had a little seashore of our own and a birch-bark navy.

You would call it Canada. We do not. We call the little ten miles square we have left of the "Grand River Country." We have the right to do that. It is ours. We have the written pledge of George III that we should have it forever as against him or his successors, and he promised to protect us in it.

We didn't think we would ever live long enough to find that a British promise was not good. An enemy's foot is on our country, and George V knows it for I told him so, but he will not lift his finger to protect us, nor will any of his ministers. One who would take away our rights is, of course, our enemy.

Do you think that any government should stop to consider whether any selfish end is to be gained or lost in the keeping of its word?

In some respects, we are just like you. We like to tell our troubles. You do that. You told us you were in great trouble a few winters ago because a great big giant with a big stick was after you. We helped you whip him. Many of our young men volunteered and many gave their lives for you. You were very willing to let them fight in the front ranks in France. Now we want to tell our troubles to you.

I do not mean that we are calling on your governments—we are tired of calling on the governments of pale-faced peoples in America and in Europe. We have tried that and found it was no use. They deal only in fine words— we want something more than that. We want justice from now on. After all that has happened to us, that is not too much to ask. You got half of your territory here by warfare upon red men, usually unprovoked, and you got about a quarter of it by bribing their chiefs, and not over a quarter of it did you get openly and fairly. You might have gotten a good share of it by fair means if you had tried.

You young people of the United States may not believe what I am saying. Do not take my word, but read your history. A good deal of true history about that has got into print now. We have a little territory left—just enough to live and die on. Don't you think your government ought to be ashamed to take that away from us by pretending it is part of theirs?

You ought to be ashamed if you let them. Before it is all gone, we mean to let you know what your governments are doing. If you are a free people, you can have your own way. The governments at Washington and Ottawa have a silent partnership of policy. It is aimed to break up every tribe of red men so as to dominate every acre of their territory. Your high officials are the nomads today—not the Red People. Your officials won't stay home.

Over in Ottawa, they call that policy "Indian advancement." Over in Washington, they call it "assimilation." We who would be the helpless victims say it is tyranny.

If this must go on to the bitter end, we would rather that you come with your guns and poison gases and get rid of us that way. Do it openly and above board. Do away with the pretense that you have the right to subjugate us to your will. Your governments do that by enforcing your alien laws upon us. That is an underhanded way. They can subjugate us if they will through the use of your law courts. But how would you like to be dragged down to Mexico, to be tried by Mexicans, and jailed under Mexican law for what you did at home?

We want none of your laws and customs that we have not willingly adopted for ourselves. We have adopted many. You have adopted some of ours—votes for women, for instance. We are as well behaved as you, and you would think so if you knew us better.

We would be happier today, if left alone, than you who call yourselves Canadians and Americans. We have no jails and do not need them. You have many jails, but do they hold all the criminals you convict? And do you convict or prosecute all your violators of the thousands of laws you have?

Your governments have lately resorted to new practices in their Indian policies. In the old days, they often bribed our chiefs to sign treaties to get our lands. Now they know that our remaining territory can easily be gotten from us by first taking our political rights away in forcing us into your citizenship, so they give jobs in their Indian offices to the bright young people among us who will take them and who, to earn their pay, say that our people wish to become citizens with you and that we are ready to have our tribal life destroyed and want your governments to do it. But that is not true.

Your governments of today learned that method from the British. The British have long practiced it on weaker peoples in carrying out their policy of subjugating the world, if they can, to British imperialism. Under cover of it, your lawmakers now assume to govern other peoples too weak to resist your courts. There are no three-mile limits or twelve-mile limits to strong governments who wish to do that.

About three winters ago, the Canadian government set out to take mortgages on farms of our returned soldiers to secure loans made to them, intending to use Canadian courts to enforce these mortgages in the name of Canadian authority within our country. When Ottawa tried that, our people resented it. We knew that would mean the end of our government. Because we did so, the Canadian government began to enforce all sorts of dominion and provincial laws over us and quartered armed men among us to enforce Canadian laws and customs upon us. We appealed to Ottawa in the name of our right as a separate people and by right of our treaties, and the door was closed in our faces. We then went to London with our treaty and asked for the protection it promised and got no attention. Then we went to the League of Nations at Geneva with its covenant to protect little peoples and to enforce respect for treaties by its members, and we spent a whole year patiently waiting but got no hearing.

To punish us for trying to preserve our rights, the Canadian government has now pretended to abolish our government by Royal Proclamation and has pretended to set up a Canadian-made government over us, composed of the few traitors among us who are willing to accept pay from Ottawa and do its bidding. Finally, Ottawa officials, under pretense of a friendly visit, asked to inspect our precious wampum belts, made by our Fathers centuries ago as records of our history, and when shown to them, these false-faced officials seized and carried away those belts as bandits take away your precious belongings. The only difference was that our aged wampum keeper did not put up his hands—our hands go up only when we address the Great Spirit. Yours go up, I hear, only when someone of you is going through the pockets of his own white brother. According to your newspapers, they are now up a good deal of the time.

The Ottawa government thought that with no wampum belts to read in the opening of our Six Nations Councils, we would give up our home rule and self-government, the victims of superstition. Any superstition of which the Grand River people have been victims are not in reverence for wampum belts, but in their trust in the honor of governments who boast of a higher civilization.

We entrusted the British, long ago, with large sums of our money to care for when we ceded back parts of their territory. They took $140,000 of

Deskaheh, Iroquois Patriot

that money seventy-five winters ago to use for their own selfish ends, and we have never been able to get it back.

Your government of the United States, I hear, has just decided to take away the political liberties of all the red men you promised to protect forever, by passing such a law through your Congress in defiance of the treaties made by George Washington. That law, of course, would mean the breaking up of the tribes if enforced. Our people would rather be deprived of their money than their political liberties—so would you.

I suppose some of you have never heard of my people before and that many of you, if you ever did, supposed that we were all long gone to our happy hunting grounds. No! There are as many of us as there were a thousand winters ago. There are more of us than there used to be and that makes a great difference in the respect we get from your governments.

I ask you a question or two. Do not hurry with your answers. Do you believe—really believe—all peoples are entitled to equal protection of international law now that you are so strong? Do you believe—really believe—that treaty pledges should be kept? Think these questions over and answer them to yourselves.

We are not as dependent in some ways as we were in the early days. We do not need interpreters now. We know your language and can understand your words for ourselves and we have learned to decide for ourselves what is good for us. It is bad for any people to take the advice of an alien people as to that.

You mothers, I hear you have a great deal to say about your government. Our mothers have always had a hand in ours. Maybe you can do something to help us now. If you white mothers are hard-hearted and will not, perhaps you boys and girls who are listening and who have loved to read stories about our people—the true ones, I mean—will help us when you grow up, if there are any of us left to be helped.

If you are bound to treat us as though we were citizens under your government, then those of your people who are land-hungry will get our farms away from us by hooks and crooks under your property laws in your courts that we do not understand and do not wish to learn. We would then be homeless and have to drift into your big cities to work for wages, to buy bread, and have to pay rent, as you call it, to live on this Earth and to live in little rooms in which we would suffocate. We would then be scattered and lost to each other and lost among so many of you. Our boys and girls would then have to intermarry with you, or not at all. If consumption [tuberculosis] took us off or if we brought no children into the world, or our children mixed with the ocean of your blood, then there would be no Iroquois left. So boys and girls, if you grow up and claim the right to live together and govern yourselves—and you ought to—and if you do not concede the same right to other peoples—and you will be strong enough to have your own way—you will be tyrants, won't you? If you do not like that word, use a better one, if you find one, but don't deceive yourselves by the words you use.

Boys, you respect your fathers because they are members of a free people and have a voice in the government over them and because they helped to make it and made it for themselves and will hand it down to you. If you knew that your fathers had nothing to do with the government they are under, but were mere subjects of others men's wills, you could not look up to them and they could not look you in the face. They would not be real men then. Neither would we.

The fathers among us have been real men. They cry out now against the injustice of being treated as something else and being called incompetents who must be governed by other people—which means the people who think that way about them.

Boys—think this over. Do it before your minds lose the power to grasp the idea that there are other peoples in this world beside your own and with an equal right to be here. You see that a people as strong as yours is a great danger to other peoples near you. Already your will comes pretty near to being law in this world where no one can whip you. Think then what it will mean if you grow up with a will to be unjust to other peoples, to believe that whatever your government does to other peoples is no crime, however wicked. I hope the Irish Americans hear that and will think about it—they used to when that shoe pinched their foot. This is the story of the Mohawks, the story of the Oneidas, of the Cayugas—I am a Cayuga, of the Onondagas, the Senecas, and the Tuscaroras. They are the Iroquois. Tell it to those who have not been listening. Maybe I will be stopped from telling it. But if I am prevented from telling it over, as I hope to do, the story will not be lost. I have already told it to thousands of listeners in Europe—it has gone into the records where your children can find it when I may be dead or be in jail for daring to tell the truth. I have told this story in Switzerland—they have free speech in little Switzerland. One can tell the truth over there in public, even if it is uncomfortable for some great people.

This story comes straight from Deskaheh, one of the chiefs of the Cayugas. I am the speaker of the Council of the Six Nations, the oldest League of Nations now existing. It was founded by Hiawatha. It is a league that is still alive and intends, as best it can, to defend the rights of the Iroquois to live under their own laws in their own little countries now left to them, to worship their Great Spirit in their own way, and to enjoy the rights that are as surely theirs as the white man's rights are his own.

If you think the Iroquois are being wronged, write letters from Canada to your ministers of parliament, and from the United States to your congressmen and tell them so. They will listen to you, for you elect them. If they are against us, ask them to tell you when and how they got the right to govern people who have no part in your government and do not live in your country but live in their own. They can't tell you that.

One word more so that you will be sure to remember our people. If it had not been for them you would not be here. If one hundred and sixty-six winters ago, our warriors had not helped the British at Québec, Québec would not have fallen to the British. The French would then have driven your English-speaking forefathers out of this land, bag and baggage. Then it would have been a French-speaking people here today, not you. That part of your history cannot be blotted out by the stealing of our wampum belts in which that is recorded.

I could tell you much more about our people, and I may some other time, if you would like to have me.

One by one, Deskaheh told of the agreements solemnly made on the sworn good faith of each of the two big governments that had guaranteed the Indian his own land, fair treatment, and independence.

Sick, fever-ridden, despairing, Deskaheh raised his voice to speak his last proud message.

The next morning, Deskaheh was in Rochester hospital. Eight weeks later he knew he was dying and asked to be taken back to Clinton Rickard's home on the Tuscarora Reservation.

While he made ready for his journey along the Milky Way to the Spirit World, his brother, wife, and children tried to cross the border at Niagara Falls to be with him, but were refused permission to do so.

On June 22, 1925, alone and with his eyes set toward the Six Nations Land he had tried to serve, he died.

White Americans and white Canadians have done little to keep the story of Deskaheh alive. Few have seen the small stone that marks his grave in the burial grounds of the Cayuga Longhouse. Fewer still care to remember his words. They make the white man uncomfortable because they bear so emphatically on contemporary thinking about the Native peoples, on proposed laws in the legislative bodies of the states and the nations that would still, despite their agreements to (in Deskaheh's words) "protect little peoples and to enforce respect for treaties," regard Indians as incompetents to be governed for their own good by wiser neighbors.

But the Iroquois remember. And when they speak of Deskaheh, the white men who know his story grow troubled, wondering if they and their governments could by some unlikely chance have dealt unjustly with a great man.

Geneva, 1977
A Report
on the Hemispheric Movement
of Indigenous Peoples

America will not begin her walk until the Indian walks. –José Martí

*We not only delivered our message on unity—we not only told them about unity—
we showed them.* –Art Solomon

I

We were in a tall, cavernous room at the United Nations, and all around
the wall and the doors there were people crowded.

The Indian delegates were all in the center, seated in rows, with long,
thin tables before them, and they had earphones on. To their right and
to their left, sitting on both sides of the room so that they faced each
other and looked over the Indian people, were the representatives of the
various governments.

Segwalise of the Haudenosaunee delegation was about to speak. He
was in front, facing us.

Next to him was Juan Condori, Aymara from Bolivia, and next to
him was José Mendoza, Guaymi from Panama. Both had spoken. This
was the last day. It had been up to them to summarize the conditions and
aspirations of their Indian peoples in South and Central America, and as
we had come to expect throughout that week, they had spoken out directly and eloquently.

Haudenosaunee and Hopi confer before the start of the conference. The international gatherings are not only a time to speak the common problems of Native peoples, they also help to reestablish the principles of unity which guide the movement.

Now it was Segwalise's turn. He did a curious thing. He didn't speak to the UN officials and he didn't speak directly to the Indian delegates, as everyone had done up to that point. No, he turned instead and faced the representatives of the various governments. He looked toward them, and he began to speak. Suddenly the focus and the tension in the room changed, and everyone felt that something real and immediate was about to happen. Segwalise was speaking to the enemy.

All week there had been pressure felt. At first slowly, but then fairly rapidly, the word had spread that in this conference no one was holding back. Finally, thoroughly and uncompromisingly it was affirmed that the Indian peoples of the American continents had not died, were not about to die, that they may now be cultures within cultures and Nations within Nations, and that their oppression may have been long and arduous—the cruelest, maybe in recorded history—but that if some things had been lost, nothing had been given up, nothing. Now they had come, one hundred thirty people, representing Hopis and Lakota, Haudenosaunee and Guaymi, Misquito and Mapuche, Northern Cheyenne and Ojibway, Aymara, Muscogee and Quichua, Schuar, Apache and Nahuatl, Quiche and Cree, and many, many more, and they had brought a message.

II

The immigration guards and officials at the Geneva airport were perplexed. The twenty-two delegates from the Six Nations (Iroquois) Confederacy, the Haudenosaunee, were lined up, passports in hand, a little tired after a nine-hour overnight flight, but now looking serious and alert as one of their passports had been handed across the glass barrier and the blonde guards with caps on were turning it over in their hands.

It was a small, brown book, covered in leather. On the cover it said: Haudenosaunee Passport.

"I don't know," one guard said. "We have to study this."

The Haudenosaunee delegation went to sit down. "Well, here we go," one man said. "We may as well start here."

The men and the women sat around. One man went to the bathroom and came back. He looked over the group casually. "What seems to be the trouble?" he said, as if he didn't know, as if there was not reason.

People smiled.

"Hey, Tim," someone else said, "did you call the Iroquois Consulate yet?"

Everyone laughed.

One of the older women repeated the antics of one of the young Indian men who had gotten off the plane pretending to be an anthropologist. "Gee," he had said, "this is how they live, eh? Do you think we could take their picture?"

That cracked everybody up.

Then the Swiss officials were back. They still seemed perplexed, but now they were offering a special entry permit. A young Swiss man was acting as interpreter.

The older Haudenosaunee called the people together. A circle was formed. The men and the women discussed the meanings and merits of this special permit.

"It seems to me," one man said, "that this permit, by virtue of being a 'special' permit, tends to negate the validity of our passport."

"That seems right," one woman said, lifting her head. "And we didn't come here to be treated differently. We came here seeking recognition."

Marci Gilbert, a youth observer from the Oglala Sioux.

Another man smiled, nodding. "That is correct," he said. "This is the whole reason that we are here."

Then a man was designated to speak for the group and he walked over to the Swiss officials. The rest of the group crowded around.

The Haudenosaunee position was delineated: the special permit could not be acceptable if in any way it negated the validity of the passport.

The Swiss officials looked perplexed. They would have to consult with their superiors, they said.

The young Swiss man who was interpreting looked nervous and fidgety. He kept looking at his watch. He was working with a reception committee member who had arranged for a bus to transport the delegations into Geneva. The bus was waiting.

Art Montour, Mohawk,
with Haudenosaunee
passport.

"It seems to me," he told the Haudenosaunee spokesman, "this is not the place for a political fight."

The man looked past him silently.

"I think the important thing is to get in," the young interpreter said.

"No," the man said softly. "The important thing is not to get in—the important thing is to make sure that every step of the way our validity as Indian nations is recognized."

The young man nodded. He looked away.

Two men from the press came. They wanted to take pictures. They wanted to know what "the trouble" was.

Soon, the officials came back. Once again the people gathered. It was to be this way: an entry permit was being offered that was the one regularly issued to passports from nations that had no formal relations with Switzerland. The Haudenosaunee had no formal relations with Geneva—

but by this act, the Swiss were recognizing the Haudenosaunee's right to travel with their own passport.

The Haudenosaunee moved away from the officials and spoke among themselves. The procedure and explanation seemed reasonable. There was agreement to accept.

Soon, the Swiss officials were handing out the passports with the permits inserted. The Haudenosaunee delegation, with the chiefs leading the way, formed a single file and passed through the gate into Switzerland.

III

There was a large circle later—and it was of all the delegations—North, Central, and South America—and one of the Lakota, Russell Means, was standing and speaking and he was slamming down forceful words, angry words.

We had been discussing the agenda for the first day—how it was to go, how much time there was, who was to speak. There was in the room and among all of us the awareness of how much there needed to be said and explained and how important it was.

Ours was a talking mission, a very complex one, and there wasn't much time. The first morning session, where a large audience and much press participation was expected, would be a crucial one. We had just become aware that the NGOs (Non-Governmental Organizations, the conference sponsors) had already scheduled several non-Indian speakers.

"I am sick and tired of this," Russell was saying, his arm extended, gesturing to the circle. "This is *our* conference. We came here, for the first time, to present our case to the world, and now we are told that we have to sit and give half our time to some damn white speakers to tell us how nice it is to have us here."

Around the room there was much nodding among silent faces. Others spoke out, mostly young men.

Juan Condori, Aymara from Bolivia, stood up. He too was adamant. "We have heard their speeches," he said. "All their polite words, all their empty words. No. I am here for my people. I am here to speak out, to tell what we are enduring. I don't have time to give."

A couple of people who had been working with the NGO committee then tried to explain the situation. It was customary, they said, that the hosts and the other observer groups represented would give welcoming addresses. There were about four such groups.

The young men, one by one, spoke again. They remained adamant. One spoke and then another, and as they went along, listening to each other, you could sense the rising circle of uncompromising anger taking hold.

NO, they were saying—all this is from the enemy. We are here to speak and at least let us do that well and in that let us not give an inch.

One of the Iroquois chiefs stood up, a quiet man, soft-spoken. "Let us not forget," he said, "that we are here as guests. In our own land we would not treat people this way. If it is the custom for these people to also speak, let us allow them their words. It doesn't seem proper that we should travel halfway around the world seeking sympathy for our cause and then begin by insulting those very people who wish to hear us."

He sat down. Again it was quiet. Many were nodding. One of the younger men stood. "If they want to hear us, let them hear us then," he said. "But don't let them start by stealing half our time."

People laughed. Other young men stood up. Once again, the anger. The young men seemed to feed off each other's anger and thus grow strong. The NGO representatives, in pretending to moderate, began to catch the hostility. It didn't seem right, and somehow it also seemed necessary—strong arguments on both sides, and you could sense the separation beginning in that room, the way that in an argument people lock into position and speak as if in different languages, and begin to forget.

Kakwirakiron stood up. He is a tall, thin man with long braids. He was there as a spokesman and representative of Kanién:ke, a Mohawk settlement in the Adirondack Mountains. There was in the room by now some apprehension and that sort of expectation within an argument when a new speaker is watched carefully to see which side he will support.

Kakwirakiron spoke casually. He said that he, too, was a young man and thus a warrior. Then he told a little bit about Kanién:ke and the kind of pressures that community had endured in the last four years of its existence. He spoke about the feelings one got from living continually in a defensive stance, not knowing on many evenings whether the morning would bring an assault by the state troopers or a few shots from some rednecks. Then he spoke about the importance of those strong feelings. "These young men," he said, "I understand them because they have been the ones in the past few years who have had the task of facing the enemy. This has been their job, and as such it is their duty to be angry, to be suspicious. Were they not this way, they would be negligent, they would not be fulfilling their obligations to the people.

"But where I come from," he said, "within the people that I come to represent, there are also old men and old women, grandparents. There are families, mothers, and there are little ones. And they also have viewpoints, feelings which must be heard, and which we must represent here. That's what we are here for. We represent the whole people—not only the warriors, not only the angry feelings. This we must keep in our minds."

Kakwirakiron sat down and around the room the people were quiet. It took a few moments, but then it seemed the anger had been focused, like the force of argument had been appropriately placed in that room. Somehow the question of time for speakers that first day got resolved. It seemed much simpler then.

IV

Phillip Deere sat in a straight-backed chair, with a red blanket folded on his lap. Now it was late at night and we were in the basement of a building in Geneva, and before him, sitting in a circle, were the group of six men who had been selected by all the delegates to be the principal speakers, to make the initial, unifying presentation, on that first day of the conference.

There were Oren Lyons, from the Iroquois Confederacy; Juan Condori, Aymara from Bolivia; José Mendoza, Guaymi from Panama; Russell Means, Lakota from the United States; and Larry Red Shirt and Francis He Crow, both also Lakotas, pipe carriers who were to open up the first day's proceedings with a Pipe Ceremony.

Phillip had his hand up and, with his forefinger, was pointing at each of the men, and he had a light smile on his face, a sort of proud and knowing smile, a confident smile.

It had been a small but important meeting. We had come together in that room to discuss the various speeches that these men would deliver on the next day, and thus eliminate any possible repetition, and yet something much stronger, something much more telling of what had been carried to Geneva had emerged.

Oren Lyons spoke first. He explained how he would address the duty of all human beings to respect not only "human rights," but the rights of all the beings of the Creation. This he went over carefully and seriously, explaining that this was the foundation for any life that would be full and decent and that could begin to guarantee the rights of future generations. Then José Mendoza spoke—and he spoke of territory, land, of the elements of the land, and how a people grew and developed according to that land and that sky, and what it offered and what it taught. He spoke of his people, the Guaymi, and of the other Indian nations, which in Panama, like in so many other countries, constituted a so-called minority within the larger state. "But we are not a minority," he said. "Within our territories we are simply us—the people—and it is only when we go outside of this—of our land–that we become 'minorities,' and then an even worse oppression begins. We become as the peasants, losing all identity, family, language, representation–to be absorbed and thus hidden, manipulated, and exploited." Then Juan Condori spoke, and he knew a thing or two about exploitation. Juan Condori is an Aymara from Bolivia where the Indian people are a majority–about four million in a country of five million–and he spoke about what it means to be an Indian and a peasant, because in his country, the two words can mean the same thing, because everyone has been displaced and the Indians, who live on but own no land, are considered inferior, less than human, by the controlling white minority.

He spoke about humiliation and poverty, and hunger–real hunger–where children don't eat, and grow malformed, and their minds don't work well, and where the parents work and work and produce so little, and even that is taken away, and all this, he said, all this is about to get even worse. A new migration, this time of racist white Rhodesians on the run from that part of the world and invited by the Bolivian government to settle a whole new region–more white settlers–sixty thousand men of arm-bearing age–ideologically trained in apartheid, tied into the development of the oppressive mining and the vast economic interests that control the country and everything going out, all the labor, all the minerals, and the land destroyed.

Russell Means spoke then. He also knew about the destruction of land, he said, referring to the Great Plains of North America. He had wanted to be last, he said, because he had a very special mission, and that was to nail the head of the monster. And the monster, the base and control of overwhelming exploitation–the force, economic and military, behind this process–this was the United States of America. It was there that the multinationals were based. It was there the counter-insurgency programs were generated. It was there where the sterilization programs were mapped out. It was there where the governments of Chile, Brazil, Guatemala, Bolivia, Panama, Venezuela, Nicaragua, Argentina, and Mexico got their military aid. And it was there where a society had been created that lived so richly, so grandiosely on the destruction of other people's lands, the exploitation of their labor, the extraction and theft of their natural resources, and finally and most fundamentally, the very rape and destruction of the Natural World–the basis of all life–the foundation, specifically, of everything the Indian represented–the sacred Mother Earth.

He wanted to make this clear, Russell said, to bring the total message back around to this, because his own people had no time left, and the Bolivians had no time left, nor the Guaymi. And in that room it became

Russell Means, Oglala Sioux.

very clear as each of the men had spoken that there had emerged no repetition but instead a sort of fusion of the various arguments, and they seemed to fold together like the cloth that wraps the Sacred Pipe. Then Larry Red Shirt spoke.

He explained the meaning of the Sacred Pipe. This was his mission—to open the ceremony and to carry and offer the Pipe. He was moved, he said, by all the words he had heard, by the strength that they represented together, how it all fit, and he knew that it was good. Then he spoke of the Pipe, of the origins of the Lakota, of the power the Pipe had and of the many manifestations he had witnessed of that power, how it had been used at Wounded Knee, and at the many trials, how he had seen, over and over, the minds of men changed by the power of that prayer and what the smoke represented.

So Phillip Deere had his hand up and his forefinger was extended, and he was pointing at each of the men, and he was smiling.

"All of you men that are going to be speaking tomorrow," he said, "you remind me of something that we do at home. And I'd like to tell you about it."

"Then he spoke of the Pipe." (left to right) David Spotted Horse, Lakota; Larry Red Shirt (holding the Pipe), Oglala Sioux; Francis He Crow, Oglala Sioux; and Philip Deere, Muskogee.

They had a ceremony at home, Phillip said, a fire-starting ceremony in which several men got around a circle, and there would be gathered also some straw or hay or wood chips, something to ignite—and then each of the men would begin. And all together they would strike flint, hitting, hitting, trying to make that spark jump.

"You men that will be speaking," Phillip said. "You remind me of those young men striking stone. Your mission is to make that spark jump—your mission is to light the fire, to ignite the hearts of all those people, of the representatives of the various countries, of the NGOs, of the mass media. You must make that spark fly.

"But it is not going to be all of you that starts that fire.

"At home, all of the young men strike the stone, over and over. Strike, strike, strike—but only one makes the spark jump. And one spark ignites the fire. So it will be tomorrow. All of you will strike. All of you will speak. And one—one of you—will ignite the fire. I know it."

65

Everyone nodded silently. Then Russell Means reached into his pocket and pulled out a butane lighter. "Here. Let's try this one too," he said.

Phillip laughed. Juan Condori laughed too, nodding, looking pleased. He turned to the interpreter. "And how is it that the Lakota say to agree?" he asked in Spanish. Then he remembered.

"Ho!" he said loudly. "Ho!"

V

Grandfather David Monongye offered a prayer and everyone surrounded him. He was wrapped in a blanket, a short, wiry man with a face full of years. Everyone's thoughts came together on the hope that what would be said that morning would be heard. The old man looked to the Earth, and he looked to the sky, and he offered his prayer to the four directions, and he spoke as only a Hopi could speak, and then the drum sounded.

People lined up and the elders took their places, the chiefs, then everyone else—the young men drumming, their voices raised high.

There were photographers all around now (they had been restricted during the prayer) and they followed to the side and behind and some ran backwards in front, stumbling over each other. The delegations marched.

Sacred Pipes leading as delegations march, "many legs and feet on hard pavement."

Grandfather David Monongye speaks to Clyde Bellecourt (with drum).

The warriors carried the drum. The women held their shawls. Some of the young people half danced, half walked, and you could see many legs and feet on the hard pavement.

"Heya . . . heya . . . heya . . . heya . . ."

I remember running in front to take a few pictures, running backwards too, and crouching down to shoot, and how strong and beautiful the people looked and how they kept on coming.

I ran way up ahead, trying to get a shot that would encompass them all, and through the lens of the camera there was the center leading, which was the men with the Pipe—the men carrying their Pipes very high and their serious proud faces—and behind them the people spreading out, coming on, and all around them and rising behind them was the early morning traffic and the city of Geneva and all those faces looking on.

Then I circled way around the back and by now the people were on the grounds of the Palais des Nations. Looking up over the backs of their heads at the windows of the United Nations buildings you could see many faces and heads sticking out, and out the doors were coming small crowds. It was obvious that the work of the whole place had been halted.

People smiled at us and a few waved.

At the entrance to the building the drum was silenced. Grandfather David offered a second prayer.

Then another song.

And from the windows and doors of the United Nations' buildings—all those people began to clap and cheer.

Then the People went inside.

VI

North and South—the American contingent. The affluence of the North; the poverty of the South. The "underdevelopment" of the South; the "overdevelopment" of the North. And what does it all mean to Indian people?

Another question: What does colonialism mean?

Colonialism is the process by which we are systematically confused. Colonialism—from the word colony: to be controlled from afar.

Confusion—an agent of control. The confusion takes many shapes and forms (gimmicks) that overlap, creating layers, many, many layers.

Western Civilization—the history of mankind since the beginning of its contradictory relationship with nature. The most basic contradiction. The history, also, thousands of years old, of the refinement of colonialist techniques. So successful that it no longer needs to regenerate the techniques, but rather, it perpetuates them.

Natural World Peoples—Nations of human beings who developed governments, religions, cultures, and economies that fit their activities to the cycles of nature. Non-colonialist by definition.

Indigenous American Peoples—Nations of human beings living on the American continent at the time of the first contact with Western civilization, the vast majority of which were and still are Natural World Peoples.

North and South—many Nations. After five hundred years of contact, many different stages of colonialism—many possibilities for confusion.

North and South—our movement: the struggle to decolonize, to break free, to stand back and view the source of the confusion, in order to develop or resume ways of living that prove to be nondestructive, healthy for the people, and at one with the creative power of nature.

VII

A press conference. Many pretty words of welcome, an equal number of insane questions.

Will they ever understand that this is not a game?

Everything was funny to them. They wanted to see the Haudenosaunee passport—take snappy front page pictures of it. They wanted to pose the people—get this angle, that angle.

This whole process of media—the distillation of information—is evidence of the insanity. Reporters who learn thousands of facts, write thousands of words, and learn nothing.

The question is not: Why do they do it? We know why they do it—for a salary, for professional recognition.

The question is: Why do they do it to themselves? Why do they care to lead such stupid, confused lives?

Today they cover the Indians; tomorrow the sewage system; the next day the high cost of food. Doesn't anything ever connect for them?

Several spokesmen tried to explain it. The meaning of sovereignty. The respect for Mother Earth. The search for integrity, the circle of life. Oppression, conquest, colonialism, exploitation. Genocide.

The reporters wanted to see the medallion around Phillip Deer's neck. "Oh, very nice," they said.

The next day we read the headlines: "INDIANS DO SCALP DANCE AT THE U.N.," and "INDIANS COME TO UNEARTH WAR HATCHET!"

VIII

Late at night in Geneva. Narrow European streets. Cobblestone. Eight, nine Indians walking in the dark, hands in pockets, hunched over shoulders, trying to guard off the chill.

It is a drizzly night, full of shadows. Small cars race by, like miniature toys.

The men walk against the wind.

One throws back his head, sideways. "In my land I would be warm" he says, the words carried by the wind.

"Ah-ha!"

"Don't talk!"

"Oh Yes!"

"And myself," says another voice, "I would have my woman rub my neck."

"Under the blanket!"

And they laugh. There's a strong wind now. Cold, cold.

On the way and there is a bar restaurant. There is a glimpse through a window—vapor on the glass—and warm, light faces inside, some noise, a crowd, beer.

They must go around the parked cars, spreading out once more. Walking against the wind, on the cobblestone street in Geneva—very far from home.

"I don't know, my brothers, sometimes it tires me—conferences, conferences—so much talk!"

"Are you asking: is it worth it?"

"I have to tell my people. They will ask me. And what will I say to them?"

"Tell them you talked for them, that you told the truth."

"That they know already."

"Oh, I see."

"What about the parasites?" they will ask. "What about our crops?"

"And what about the uncle—the one with the bad arm. Can you fix him up?"

Laughter. Pleasant, knowing laughter.

"Brother. And will Geneva buy me a pair of shoes?"

Laughter, laughter.

"Brothers, we came together. That is something."

"And it must be said, one and another time. Say it, say it, say it—let the words go out."

"It makes a difference. Look at brother Constantino—it got him out of a cell."

"If enough of us say it—often enough—we let it loose. It will carry itself."

Long, rounded curves and rock walls defining the road. Clean streets, glistening. Geneva—a city of precision. Clockwork, music boxes, and intricate banking schemes. Money and order, where people are assumed to be honest, or scared, and nobody collects your ticket on the bus. The police are swift, and the people line up automatically.

Once, they were Lake Dwellers—the original inhabitants—a tribal people with relatives all along the Alpine region. Skilled agriculturalists, fishermen, hunters. Highly developed weaving and ornamental arts—peaceful, prosperous, with many village clusters around a single lake. Then the Celts invaded; then the Etruscans. And finally, the Romans. The Romans eradicated the local cultures, built roads, changed the languages, brought diseases, conscripted the men, enslaved the people, collected tribute. Later came wars with the Franks, with the Allemany—out of this the Swiss were formed. A strange breed. Sturdy. Gracious. Hardworking. Stingy. Cosmopolitan. European.

A car rounds a corner and surprises the walking figures. It honks. The men form a single file at the edge. The driver, a man, is signaling angrily, honks again, speeds on.

70

"Just like at home. Ay!"

The men laugh.

"They do that, brothers, in my country. They push us to the side and drive their big cars through, through, through!"

The Aymara pretends to hold a steering wheel, pushing, pushing.

Now he is angry. "They think we are beasts!"

"They do. They do."

The Indian people of Brazil could not come. There they are considered as children, minors who must travel with a guardian, a white Brazilian.

"Do you need a guardian, my brother?"

The men laugh, sadly.

"You know. In my country they call us pigs. It is the same as saying Indian!"

November 1980: A Mayan delegate testifies before the Fourth Russell Tribunal on the Indians of the Americas. The Mayas—the largest Native nation in Central America—are undergoing intense oppression at the hands of Western materialism-imperialism. Three years after Geneva, the Fourth Russell Tribunal served to document the specific cases of oppression of Native peoples. Mayan delegates were murdered on their return to Guatemala.

Akwesasne Notes photo: Dick Bancroft

Haudenosaunee Delegation: (left to right) Back row: Artley Skenandore, Oneida; Frank Abrams, Seneca; Stuart Patterson, Tuscarora; Leo Henry, Tuscarora. Middle row: Aaron Oakes, Mohawk; Art Montour, Mohawk; Dan Bomberry, Cayuga; Bruce Elijah, Oneida; Loran Thompson, Mohawk; Leon Shenandoah, Onondaga, Audrey Shenandoah, Onondaga; Corbett Sundown, Seneca; Oren Lyons, Onondaga; Jimmy Leaf, Cayuga. Kneeling: Lee Lyons, Seneca; Louie Thompson, Mohawk; Francis Boots, Mohawk; and Ray Halbritter, Oneida.

"If our brothers from Brazil, if they could come . . . how much they could say!"

"The same as you and me!"

The nine figures are walking in a huddle, in the shadows.

One man sings a song—a lilting, lifting song.

Two men walk comfortably with their arms around each others' shoulders.

"Brothers, brothers. I love you all—but I don't want to see you again."

"What's that you say?"

"We grow strong together. There is no doubt. We share it. Send someone else next time."

"'Yes. That is the thing."

"Sing another song then. Sing, will you. Sing."

IX

Testimony was being taken, and the Bolivians were in a cluster when they saw him.

"There he is. That's him!"

"Duck your head down!"

Across the room, over the heads of the other delegates, was a young photographer. He was focusing his camera on them, trying to get frontal face shots.

"Look down at your notes."

The photographer lowered his camera. He signaled across the room to another man, who also held a camera. The second man went outside, and the first one lit a cigarette. Then he too went outside.

The Bolivian military attaché had come that day. He was flanked by a staff of four—two men and two women—all well dressed. They took careful notes.

One by one the governments had heard. Something was being said over here that no North, Central, or South American government state could live with comfortably.

The Indian people were claiming their land.

The Indian people were claiming their right to exist as Indian people, wherever they might be.

The Indian people were claiming their right to continue to live a Way of Life that had proven itself healthy and adequate for human beings.

This was the message of this UN conference. And if it was a message that couldn't be delivered in its totality, it was because it is not a message of words only. It is about a real world, and about a real people—and in Geneva, after five hundred years of contact, it was a message about how these people, by no means perfect, but with a sane, healthy vision of existence, guided by concepts of unity and reciprocity, the positive values of non-accumulation of wealth and, most fundamentally, an all-encompassing comprehension of how the life-force manifests itself in all the beings of the Creation—how these peoples sometimes gradually but oftentimes suddenly found and find themselves barraged by missionaries, soldiers of fortune, educators, economic developers, armies, and all manner of confusing gimmicks—and one by one they are extinguished, they disappear—they fight; they kill themselves; they get contaminated; they are assimilated; they survive; they unite.

And over and over this story had told itself, was documented, was specified. And it was the same in the Bolivian highlands as it was in Pine Ridge in South Dakota; in the Paraguayan Chaco as in Akwesasne. And the people could see that now, there was no doubt now.

The governments of North, Central, and South America find much to fear in this new unity.

For the South and Central American governments, who make a studied habit of criticizing that "colossus of the North"—United States imperialism—and yet take its money and military aid for their own colonizing expansions, this was unacceptable.

Mexico, Nicaragua, Venezuela, and Bolivia found ways to pressure the Indian delegates from within their political borders.

I remember a couple of tall, well-dressed, mustachioed Mexicans cornering young Natalio, a Nahuatl delegate. They loomed over him, with serious, threatening faces.

The Mexican government will not have it said it mistreats "our" Indians, they said.

"Furthermore," one of the men said, "there are only eight million Indians in our country—not twelve million as your report said."

Natalio shrugged. "You know these figures are hard to ascertain."

"Eight million!"

Natalio looked away.

"And another thing we want mentioned: the Indians fought for Mexico, in many wars."

"I know," Natalio said. "I know we did."

The Nicaraguan ambassador to Geneva tried to call one of the Misquitos out of a meeting. The Indian wouldn't go.

"This is friendly," the ambassador sent word.

They met for dinner one night. Our position is very clear, the Misquito said. We are one hundred thousand people, within our territories. We are not you and you are not us.

One day the Yecuana from Venezuela looked troubled, withdrawn. "They are pressuring me," he said. "There are threats."

And of course Bolivia—where the struggle is intensifying and the Indian people have vowed to dust off their old, hidden rifles because no longer can they tolerate the humiliation and oppression—and this is it: if the Rhodesians move in, apartheid becomes official.

In the United States, the word is out that Russell Means will again be imprisoned—his parole broken too blatantly, too politically. The court won't tolerate it.

So it goes. And some others too, that one cannot mention.

And over there are the photographers again, during the Legal Commission testimony. They come in opposite sides and set up to photograph the Aymaras and Quichuas from Bolivia.

The Aymaras look down. But then: "Brothers," one says, "if they want my picture, they can have it."

He looks up, straight at the photographers. Under his breath he says, "It is going to take more than cameras to shut me up."

And another one looks up—a dark face, with red, tired eyes. "They'll have to cut my heart out," he says. "Truly they will."

Dan Bomberry, of the Haudenosaunee Delegation, is walking around, He too carries a camera, this one with a long lens. The Aymaras call him over. They want him to shoot the photographers.

Bomberry walks away, crouches down, shoots. He shoots again and again, from the sides, from the front. And the photographers shoot back at them—at the Aymaras and Quichuas, at the other delegates.

Bomberry then shoots the Bolivian military attaché and his staff. They glare at him scoffingly.

Stephen Gaskin, an independent observer from The Farm, a U.S. self-sufficient community, is also recruited. He has a small, dinky camera, but he wields it with flair, joining the skirmish, shooting, shooting.

Pretty soon the two photographers retreat. The Aymaras are laughing, laughing. But the Bolivian military man is still looking out, silently, angrily.

X

We were in a tall, cavernous room at the United Nations, and this was the last day. Segwalise of the Haudenosaunee Delegation was about to speak.

It had been a long week, a week of sleeping three, maybe four hours a night, a week of transatlantic flights and hurried breakfasts and the ever-present need to say things right. A week of pressure and energy—the constant energy. Because something had happened in this conference, something was helping. People were locking together, and one after another they had transcended themselves, as if they knew, finally, that the truth, once you know it, carries with it an awesome, beautiful obligation—that there is no going back.

We were tired. Everyone was tired, but I don't mean tired in that way that one begins to forget things. No, rather I mean tired in that way that all your emotional reserves, your usual, everyday customary buffers have been used up, and so whatever is around you enters your being and flows through you and becomes part of what you are, and Segwalise was groping for words.

"I want to say," he began slowly, and he looked toward the Bolivian military people, to the Venezuelan, the Nicaraguan, the Panamanian government representatives. This was for them. It was from us to them. "As a person who has helped work to achieve this time, this first time when our people have come here as one people of the Western Hemisphere to talk to the world and try to explain the conditions that we face, that what I have seen in the past year of work on this is that there has been an organic growth, as when you put that seed into the Earth and you know that the various things of the Earth work together with that seed to bring about a good thing for the life of all the people.

"That cycle has been going on since the time that this place began. My deepest concern in this work has always been that unfortunately the people who occupy our part of the world with us, for whatever reasons seem to have a vicious strain in them. It may be because their guilt is so overwhelming about how they treat us, that sometimes they have to murder us, or jail us, or assassinate our leaders, or carry on acts against our people.

"I hope that those of you who sit in this room with us, as representatives of the co-occupiers of our part of the world, you will be able to think a little bit about our lives, our aspirations, our wants, our desires, before you send your final reports home. Before you send your reports home that may cause a . . . a . . . death. . . ."

And here Segwalise had to stop—and we all stopped. And he had to fight for words, because he was choked up, and in that room the tears began to flow.

". . . That may cause a death among a people that I have come to know and love. Because if one of them disappears from the face of this Earth, because they came here to speak the truth about the conditions we live in, and the things we have to face, the people who remember that man's death will be coming after you . . . ."

Wild applause, everyone on their feet.

"We have a chance," Segwalise said, "in the Western Hemisphere, to work together as human beings, as people. And as the Native people of this land we have come to this World Council to try to show you that even through all the things you have done to us, we still have a feeling of kindness in our hearts.

"But if you do not stop, if you continue, do not be surprised by the reaction the people reap upon you. What you create today, how you say it, how you feel it, how you manifest it as you walk upon the Earth, comes back to you. It always goes in a full circle.

"It always comes back. And if you find it in your hearts to be human beings, to give a little bit of life, a little bit of consideration for us as human beings, then it comes back. And that's the balance of this Way of Life that we carry on our side of the world. And we always try, we always try to put it into your hearts and into your minds. Don't let your economic interests, don't let your military interests override your humanity. Because we are not going to go away, we are not going to disappear.

"We are going to be here for a very long time. And every morning when you wake up, somehow, someplace, somewhere, you are going to have to face us again. So let's try in your reports home, and in our reports home, to look for ways that we can get back to the good life in the Western Hemisphere."

EPILOGUE

José Mendoza, the Guaymi delegate came back with us for a visit. This was a few days after the conference, and we were sitting in one of the hill-top cabins at *Notes*. Mendoza looked up from the table and said: "I must confess I am truly confused."

It was his first visit to North America. We had flown into Syracuse and after a day's rest at Onondaga, had traveled the fast, angry highways north to Akwesasne.

"This is a strange land," Mendoza kept saying.

Late at night he asked the crucial question: "Tell me," he said, "in this country, just how does one know who are the Indians?"

A big question—a big, big question.

In his country, Mendoza said, Indians don't drive pick-up trucks; Indians don't work at big-money jobs. Part of that is the poverty of the Panamanian society, he said. But also, it is widely recognized in the communities that once you begin to move into that life you cease to be an Indian.

This began a long discussion that night, around the table. We talked about the People—how they defined themselves, what kind of principles they lived by. Then we talked about poverty and wealth—how they were two sides of the same force, how they could be used as instruments of oppression.

We talked about North and South, about the attempt to live an integral life, and we came to understand how the way of life of Indian people is just as perversely (and maybe even more thoroughly) oppressed by wealth as it is by forced poverty.

The next morning there was to be a report on Geneva in the Longhouse at Akwesasne. I stayed behind in the mountains to finish up some work, but Mendoza went along.

The Longhouse was crowded with people—and, after the reports, which were delivered in Mohawk, there was much dancing and singing and a feast.

Mendoza came back late that night. He was smiling. "The confusion has flown away from me," he said. "I feel good tonight. Down there, at the Casa Larga—that was just like being home!"

José Barreiro (Ismaelillo)
associate editor at *Akwesasne Notes* (1975-1984)
presently senior editor at *Indian Country Today*

A Basic Call to Consciousness

The Haudenosaunee Address to the Western World

Geneva, Switzerland
Autumn 1977

Introduction

It was not long ago that the Haudenosaunee, or Six Nations, were a powerful people, occupying a vast territory stretching from Vermont to Ohio, and from present day Québec to Tennessee. At the period of first contact early during the seventeenth century, the Haudenosaunee occupied hundreds of towns and villages throughout the country.

Haudenosaunee means "people who build," and it is the proper name of the people of the Longhouse. The early history, history before the Indo-Europeans came, explains that there was a time when the peoples of the North American forest experienced war and strife. It was during such a time that there came into this land one who carried words and plans of peace. That one would come to be called Peacemaker.

The Peacemaker came to the people with a message that human beings should cease abusing one another. He stated that humans are capable of reason, that through the power of reason all men desire peace, and that it is necessary that people organize to ensure that peace will be possible among the people who walk about on the Earth. That was the original word about laws—laws were originally made to prevent the abuse of humans by other humans.

The Peacemaker traveled among the people, going from nation to nation, seeking those who would take up this way of peace, offering with it a way of reason and power. He journeyed first among the Kanien'kehá:ka—the People of Flint Stone (Mohawks) —where he sought to speak to the most dangerous of these people, offering them his message.

He traveled for a long time among the Mohawks; the People of Standing Stone (the Oneidas), the People of the Hills (Onondagas), the People of the Swamp (Cayugas), and the People of the Great Hills (Senecas). Eventually, those five nations were the initial ones to take up the offer of peace. The nations gathered together in a council, and there they set down the principles of what is called the Kaianere'kó:wa, or the Great Law of Peace.

It is impossible to overstate the power of thought that emerges from that document. Today, it is almost impossible for us to recreate the scene of its birth. But centuries ago, a Natural World people gathered together at the head of a lake in the center of North America's then virgin forest, and there they counseled. The principles that emerged are unequaled in any political document that has yet emerged. They evolved a law that recognized that vertical hierarchy creates conflicts, and they dedicated the superbly complex organization of their society to function to prevent the rise internally of hierarchy.

Secondly, they looked into their own histories to discover the things that cause conflict among people. They saw, for example, that peoples sometimes struggle over hunting territories, and they did a curious thing. They abolished the significance of such territories. and guaranteed the safety of anyone entering the country of the Haudenosaunee. And they established universal laws about the treatment and taking of game, because the taking of game sometimes caused conflicts. In the country of the Haudenosaunee, all people were free, all had a right to protection under what the Peacemaker called the Great Tree of Peace.

The basic principles of peace went further than the simple absence of conflict. An ordered society that has the capability of protecting people against abuse and, at the same time, is dedicated to a containment of hierarchy, is a complex society. The People of the Longhouse sought to carry the principles of peace far from the council fires, into every dwelling in the country of the Haudenosaunee. Thus does the Great Law establish more than a code of conduct—it is also the beginning point for the modern clans. It embodies the foundations of all the customs of holding meetings, of exchanging messages on wampums, and of assigning titles to leaders.

The Haudenosaunee raised their children from the cradleboard to be participants in the culture. The ways of the People of the Longhouse have always been powerfully spiritual in nature, and it is true that the government, the economy, everything that is Haudenosaunee has deep spiritual roots.

The papers that follow are the position papers that were presented by the Haudenosaunee to the Non-Governmental Organizations of the United Nations in Geneva, Switzerland, in September 1977. The Non-Governmental Organizations had called for papers that describe the conditions of oppression suffered by Native people under three subject headings, with supportive oral statements to be given to the commissions. The Haudenosaunee, the traditional Six Nations Council at Onondaga, sent forth three papers that constitute an abbreviated analysis of Western history and call for a consciousness of the sacred Web of Life in the universe.

It is a call that can be expected to be both ignored and misunderstood for some period of time. But the position papers themselves are absolutely unique—they constitute a political statement, presented to a representative world body, pointing to the destruction of the Natural World and the

Natural World peoples as the clearest indicator that human beings are in trouble on this planet. It is a call to a basic consciousness that has ancient roots and ultramodern, even futuristic, manifestations.

It is a statement that points to the fact that humans are abusing one another, that they are abusing the planet they live on, and that they are even abusing themselves. It is a message, certainly the first ever delivered to a world body, that identifies the process of that abuse as Western civilization as a whole way of life—and acknowledges the immense complexity implied by that statement.

What is presented here is nothing less audacious than a cosmogony of the industrialized world presented by the most politically powerful and independent non-Western political body surviving in North America. It is, in a way, the modern world through Pleistocene eyes.

Scholars and casual readers alike should question the significance, in the age of the neutron bomb, Watergate, and nuclear energy plant proliferation, of a statement by a North American Indian people. But there is probably some argument to be made for the appropriateness of such a statement at this time. Most of the world's professed traditions are fairly recent in origin. Islam is perhaps fifteen hundred years old; Christianity claims a two thousand-year history; Judaism is perhaps two thousand years older than Christianity.

But the Native people can probably lay claim to a tradition that reaches back to at least the end of the Pleistocene, and which, in all probability, goes back much farther than that.

There is some evidence that humanoid creatures have been present on the Earth for at least two million years, and that humans who looked very much like us were in evidence in the Northern Hemisphere at least as long ago as the second interglacial period. People who are familiar with the Haudenosaunee beliefs will recognize that modern scientific evidence shows that the Native customs of today are not markedly different from those practiced by ancient peoples at least seventy thousand years ago. Indeed, if an Iroquois traditionalist were to seek a career in the study of Pleistocene Man, he may find that he already knows more about the most ancient belief systems than do the modern scholars.

Be that as it may, the Haudenosaunee position is derived from a philosophy that sees The People with historical roots that extend back tens of thousands of years. It is a geological kind of perspective, which sees modern man as an infant, occupying a very short space of time in an incredibly long spectrum. It is the perspective of the oldest elder looking into the affairs of a young child and seeing that he is committing incredibly destructive folly. It is, in short, the statement of a people who are ageless but who trace their history as a people to the very beginning of time. And they are speaking, in this instance, to a world that dates back its existence from a little over five hundred years ago, and perhaps, in many cases, much more recently than that.

And it is, to our knowledge, the very first such sentence to be issued by a Native nation. What follows are not research products of psychologists, historians, or anthropologists. The papers that follow are the first authentic analysis of the modern world ever committed to writing by an official body of Native people.

Spiritualism
The Highest Form of Political
Consciousness
The Haudenosaunee Message
to the Western World

The Haudenosaunee, or the Six Nations Iroquois Confederacy, has existed on this land since the beginning of human memory. Our culture is among the most ancient, continuously existing cultures in the world. We still remember the earliest doings of human beings. We remember the original instructions of the Creators of Life on this place we call Ionkhi'nisténha onhwéntsia–Mother Earth. We are the spiritual guardians of this place. We are the Onkwehón:we–the Real People.

In the beginning, we were told that the human beings who walk about the Earth have been provided with all the things necessary for life. We were instructed to carry a love for one another, and to show a great respect for all the beings of this Earth. We are shown that our life exists with the tree life, that our well-being depends on the well-being of the vegetable life, that we are close relatives of the four-legged beings. In our ways, spiritual consciousness is the highest form of politics.

Ours is a Way of Life. We believe that all living things are spiritual beings. Spirits can be expressed as energy forms manifested in matter. A blade of grass is an energy form manifested in matter–grass matter. The spirit of the grass is that unseen force that produces the species of grass, and it is manifest to us in the form of real grass.

All things of the world are real, material things. The Creation is a true, material phenomenon, and the Creation manifests itself to us through reality. The spiritual universe, then, is manifest to man as the Creation, the Creation that supports life. We believe that man is real, a part of the Creation, and that his duty is to support life in conjunction with the other beings. That is why we call ourselves Onkwehón:we—Real People.

The original instructions direct that we who walk about on the Earth are to express a great respect, an affection, and a gratitude toward all the spirits that create and support life. We give a greeting and thanksgiving to the many supporters of our own lives—the corn, beans, squash, the winds, the sun. When people cease to respect and express gratitude for these many things, then all life will be destroyed, and human life on this planet will come to an end.

Our roots are deep in the lands where we live. We have a great love for our country, for our birthplace is there. The soil is rich from the bones of thousands of our generations. Each of us was created in those lands, and it is our duty to take great care of them, because from these lands will spring the future generations of the Onkwehón:we. We walk about with a great respect, for the Earth is a very sacred place.

We are not a people who demand or ask anything of the Creators of Life; instead, we give greetings and thanksgiving that all the forces of life are still at work. We deeply understand our relationship to all living things. To this day, the territories we still hold are filled with trees, animals, and the other gifts of the Creation. In these places we still receive our nourishment from our Mother Earth.

We have seen that not all people of the Earth show the same kind of respect for this world and its beings. The Indo-European people who have colonized our lands have shown little respect for the things that create and support life. We believe that these people ceased their respect for the world a long time ago. Many thousands of years ago, all the people of the world believed in the same Way of Life, that of harmony with the universe. All lived according to the Natural Ways.

Around ten thousand years ago, peoples who spoke Indo-European languages lived in the area that today we know as the Steppes of Russia. At that time, they were a Natural World people who lived off the land. They had developed agriculture, and it is said that they had begun the practice of animal domestication. It is not known that they were the first people in the world to practice animal domestication. The hunters and gatherers who roamed the area probably acquired animals from the agricultural people and adopted an economy based on the herding and breeding of animals.

Herding and breeding of animals signaled a basic alteration in the relationship of humans to other life forms. It set into motion one of the true revolutions in human history. Until herding, humans depended on nature for the reproductive powers of the animal world. With the advent of herding, humans assumed the functions that had for all time been the functions of the spirits of the animals. Sometime after this happened, history records the first appearance of the social organization known as "patriarchy."

The area between the Tigris and Euphrates Rivers was the homeland, in ancient times, of various peoples, many of whom spoke Semitic languages. The Semitic people were among the first in the world to develop irrigation technology. This development led to the early development of towns, and eventually cities. The manipulation of the waters, another form of spirit life, represented another way in which humans developed a technology that reproduced a function of nature.

Within these cultures, stratified hierarchical social organization crystallized. The ancient civilizations developed imperialism, partly because of the very nature of cities. Cities are obviously population concentrations. Most importantly though, they are places that must import the material needs of this concentration from the countryside. This means that the Natural World must be subjugated, extracted from, and exploited in the interest of the city. To give order to this process, the Semitic world developed early codes of law. They also developed the idea of monotheism to serve as a spiritual model for their material and political organization.

Much of the history of the ancient world recounts the struggles between the Indo-Europeans and the Semitic peoples. Over a period of several millennia, the two cultures clashed and blended. By the second millennia BC, some Indo-Europeans, most specifically the Greeks, had adopted the practice of building cities, thus becoming involved in the process they named "civilization."

Both cultures developed technologies peculiar to civilizations. The Semitic peoples invented kilns, which enabled the creation of pottery for trade and the storage of surpluses. These early kilns eventually evolved into ovens that could generate enough heat to smelt metals, notably copper, tin, and bronze. The Indo-Europeans developed a way of smelting iron.

Rome fell heir to these two cultures and became the place where the final meshing occurs. Rome is also the true birth place of Christianity. The process that has become the culture of the West is historically and linguistically a Semitic/Indo-European culture, but has been commonly termed the Judeo-Christian tradition.

Christianity was an absolutely essential element in the early development of this kind of technology. Christianity advocated only one God. It was a religion that imposed itself exclusive of all other beliefs. The local people of the European forests were a people who believed in the spirits of the forests, waters, hills, and the land. Christianity attacked those beliefs and effectively despiritualized the European world. The Christian peoples, who possessed superior weaponry and a need for expansion, were able to militarily subjugate the tribal peoples of Europe.

The availability of iron led to the development of tools that could cut down the forest, the source of charcoal to make more tools. The newly cleared land was then turned by the newly developed iron plow that was, for the first time, pulled by horses. With that technology, many fewer people would work much more land, and many other people were effectively displaced to become soldiers and landless peasants. The rise of that technology ushered in the Feudal Age and eventually made possible the rise of new cities and growing trade. It also spelled the beginning of the end of the European forest, although that process took a long time to complete.

The eventual rise of cities and the concurrent rise of the European state created the thrust of expansion and a search for markets that led men, such as Columbus, to set sail across the Atlantic. The development of sailing vessels and navigation technologies made the European "discovery" of the Americas inevitable.

The Americas provided Europeans a vast new area for expansion and material exploitation. Initially, the Americas provided new materials and even finished materials for the developing world economy that was based on Indo-European technologies. European civilization has a history of rising and falling as its technologies reach their material and cultural limits. The finite natural world has always provided a kind of built-in contradiction to Western expansion.

The Indo-Europeans attacked every aspect of North America with unparalleled zeal. The Native people were ruthlessly destroyed because they were an unassimilable element to the civilizations of the West. The forests provided materials for larger ships, the land was fresh and fertile for agricultural surpluses, and some areas provided sources of slave labor for the conquering invaders. By the time of the Industrial Revolution in the mid-nineteenth century, North America was already a leader in the area of the development of extractive technology.

The hardwood forests of the Northeast were not cleared for the purpose of providing farmlands. Those forests were destroyed to create charcoal for the fires of the iron smelters and blacksmiths. By the 1890s, the West had turned to coal, a fossil fuel, to provide the energy necessary for the many new forms of machinery that had been developed. During the first half of the twentieth century, oil had replaced coal as a source of energy.

Over the years many peoples of the world have come into alliances with the movement for the recognition of Native nations. Spiritual peoples, in particular, have no difficulty understanding the quest for peace and the wish to respect all beings in the Sacred Web of Life. The Most Venerable Nichidatsu Fujii (1885-1995), Japanese Buddhist teacher, rode his wheel chair on the Longest Walk. Speaking on the U.S. Capitol steps at the conclusion of the Longest Walk, July 16, 1978, Nichidatsu Fujii said, "The religious faith that the Native Americans have carried down to this day will be the fountainhead for creating lasting peace in the future."

Akwesasne Notes photo: Jean-Francois Graunard

The Western culture has been horribly exploitative and destructive of the Natural World. Over one hundred forty species of birds and animals were utterly destroyed since the European arrival in the Americas, largely because they were unusable in the eyes of the invaders. The forests were leveled, the waters polluted, the Native people subjected to genocide. The vast herds of herbivores were reduced to mere handfuls; the buffalo nearly became extinct. Western technology and the people who have employed it have been the most amazingly destructive forces in all of human history. No natural disaster has ever destroyed as much. Not even the Ice Ages counted as many victims.

But like the hardwood forests, the fossil fuels are also finite resources. As the second half of the twentieth century progressed, the people of the West began looking to other forms of energy to motivate their technology. Their eyes settled on atomic energy, a form of energy production that has by-products that are the most poisonous substances ever known to man.

Today, man is facing the very survival of the human species. The way of life known as "Western Civilization" is on a death path, and its culture has no viable answers. When faced with the reality of its own destructiveness, Western civilization can only go forward into areas of more efficient destruction. The appearance of plutonium on this planet is the clearest of signals that our species is in trouble. It is a signal that most Westerners have chosen to ignore.

The air is foul, the waters poisoned, the trees dying, the animals are disappearing. We think even the systems of weather are changing. Our ancient teaching warned us that if man interfered with the natural laws, these things would come to be. When the last of the Natural Way of Life is gone, all hope for human survival will be gone with it. And our Way of Life is fast disappearing, a victim of the destructive processes.

The other position papers of the Haudenosaunee have outlined our analysis of economic and legal oppression. But our essential message to the world is a basic call to consciousness. The destruction of the Native cultures and people is the same process that has destroyed and is destroying life on this planet. The technologies and social systems that have destroyed the animals and the plant life are also destroying the Native people. And that process is Western civilization.

We know that there are many people in the world who can quickly grasp the intent of our message. But experience has taught us that there are few who are willing to seek out a method for moving toward any real change. But if there is to be a future for all beings on this planet, we must begin to seek the avenues of change.

The processes of colonialism and imperialism that have affected the Haudenosaunee are but a microcosm of the processes affecting the world. The system of reservations employed against our people is a microcosm of the system of exploitation used against the whole world. Since the time of Marco Polo, the West has been refining a process that mystified the peoples of the Earth.

The majority of the world does not find its roots in Western culture or traditions. The majority of the world finds its roots in the Natural World, and it is the Natural World and the traditions of the Natural World that must prevail if we are to develop truly free and egalitarian societies.

It is necessary at this time to begin a process of critical analysis of the West's historical processes, to seek out the actual nature of the roots of the exploitative and oppressive conditions that are forced upon humanity. At the same time, as we gain an understanding of those processes, we must reinterpret that history to the people of the world. It is the people of the West, ultimately, who are most oppressed and exploited. They are burdened by the weight of centuries of racism, sexism, and ignorance, which has rendered their people insensitive to the true nature of their lives.

We must all consciously and continuously challenge every model, every program, and every process that the West tries to force upon us. Paulo Friere wrote in his book *The Pedagogy of the Oppressed* that it is the nature of the oppressed to imitate the oppressor, and by such actions try to gain relief from the oppressive condition. We must learn to resist that response to oppression.

The people who are living on this planet need to break with the narrow concept of human liberation and begin to see liberation as something that needs to be extended to the whole of the Natural World. What is needed is the liberation of all the things that support life—the air, the waters, the trees—all the things that support the sacred Web of Life.

We feel that the Native peoples of the Western Hemisphere can continue to contribute to the survival potential of the human species. The majority of our peoples still live in accordance with the traditions that find their roots in the Mother Earth. But the Native peoples have need of a forum where our voice can be heard. And we need alliances with other peoples of the world to assist in our struggle to regain and maintain our ancestral lands and to protect the Way of Life we follow.

We know that this is a very difficult task. Many nation states may feel threatened by the position that the protection and liberation of Natural World peoples and cultures represent, a progressive direction that must be integrated into the political strategies of people who seek to uphold the dignity of man. But that position is growing in strength, and it represents a necessary strategy in the evolution of progressive thought.

The traditional Native peoples hold the key to the reversal of the processes in Western civilization that hold the promise of unimaginable future suffering and destruction. Spiritualism is the highest form of political consciousness. And we, the Native peoples of the Western Hemisphere, are among the world's surviving proprietors of that kind of consciousness. We are here to impart that message.

The Obvious Fact of Our Continuing Existence
Legal History of the Haudenosaune

Since the beginning of human time, the Haudenosaunee have occupied the distinct territories that we call our homelands. That occupation has been both organized and continuous. We have long defined the borders of our country, have long maintained the exclusive use–right of the areas within those borders–and have used those territories as the economic and cultural definitions of our nation. The Haudenosaunee are a distinct people, with our own laws, customs, territories, political organization, and economy. In short, the Haudenosaunee, or Six Nations, fits in every way every definition of nationhood.

Ours is one of the most complex social-political structures still functioning in the world. The Haudenosaunee Council is also one of the most ancient, continuously functioning governments anywhere on this planet. Our society is one of the most complex anywhere. From our social and political institutions has come inspiration for some of the most vital institutions and political philosophies of the modern world.

The Haudenosaunee are governed by a constitution known among Europeans as the Constitution of the Six Nations and to the Haudenosaunee as the Kaianere'kó:wa, or the Great Law of Peace. It is the oldest functioning document in the world that has contained a recognition of the freedoms the Western democracies recently claim as their own: the freedom of speech, freedom of religion, and the rights of women to participate in government. The concepts of separation of powers in government and of checks and balances of power within governments are traceable to our constitution. They are ideas learned by the colonists as the result of contact with North American Native people, specifically the Haudenosaunee.[1]

The philosophies of the socialist world, too, are to some extent traceable to European contact with the Haudenosaunee. Lewis Henry Morgan noted the economic structure of the Haudenosaunee, which he termed both primitive and communistic.[2] Karl Marx used Morgan's observations for the development of a model for a classless, post-capitalist society.[3] The modern world has been greatly influenced by the fact of our existence.

It may seem strange, at this time, that we are here, asserting the obvious fact of our continuing existence. For countless centuries, the fact of our existence was unquestioned, and for all honest human beings, it remains unquestioned today. We have existed since time immemorial. We have always conducted our own affairs from our territories under our own laws and customs. We have never, under those laws and customs, willingly or fairly surrendered either our territories or our freedoms. Never, in the history of the Haudenosaunee, have our people or our government sworn allegiance to a European sovereign. In that simple fact lies the roots of our oppression as a people and the purpose of our journey here before the world community.

The problems incurred in the recent "legal history" of the Haudenosaunee began long before European contact with Native people. It began, at least, with the rise of a system called feudalism in Europe, for the only law that the colonizing countries of Europe ever recognized was feudal law, a fact that they have obscured from their own people as well as from Native people for many centuries. That fact, however, remains the essential reality of the legal relationships that exist between Native peoples and Indo-European societies.

Feudal society in Europe appears to have arisen as the result of a number of conditions that existed following the dissolution of the Roman Empire. It was based on a system by which rulers of warrior castes became strong enough to demand and extract fealty from warriors. There arose, generally, an administrative center, usually a castle, and around these were agricultural people who were usually protected from outside aggression by their "lord," the sovereign of the manor. It appears likely that new technologies arose that created economies that made the feudal society both possible and perhaps even inevitable in Europe.

The feudal lord often held dictatorial power over his "subjects," especially the peasants. Military protection was necessary because of the continuous state of "feuding" among the various lords. The "peaceful people," or peasants, were caught in the middle. The land and everything on it,

including the animals, plants, and people, were under the domination or dominion of the feudal "lord." This lord demanded loyalty and a part of the peasant's crops, as well as some of his or her labor. Feudalism could be far more brutal and humiliating than is outlined in many histories. Some feudal lords exercised what was called "the right of the first night," a custom that referred to the right of a lord to a peasant's bride.

Prior to the rise of feudalism, it is fair to state that most of the agricultural people of Europe were local tribesmen of various kinds. Feudalism imposed the concept of sovereign, dictatorial rulers whose rule was imposed by military might and gave rise to the true European peasantry.

The crystallization of centralized executive power served to separate civilized societies from primitive societies. It is immaterial whether such controls are located in a feudal castle or in the executive offices of the capitals of nation states. The appearance of the hierarchical state marks the transition of food cultivators in general to the more specific definition contained in the concepts of peasantry. When the cultivator becomes dependent upon and integrated into a society in which he is subject to the demands of people who are defined by a class other than his own, he becomes appropriately termed a peasant.[4]

The state of a medieval European peasant was not a pleasant one. Peasants have no rights, save those granted by their lord. They cannot own the land as a people. Only the sovereign owns or possesses sovereignty. Peasants were often treated as chattel. They were bought, sold, and inherited with the land. They were a people who had been dispossessed of their freedom. At some points in history, the tribal peoples of Europe became peasants through a combination of forces, the most direct being military pressure.

A peasant is not a member of a true community of people. His society is incomplete without the town or city. It is trade with the town or city, an economic relationship, that defines the early stages of peasantry. As trade becomes more necessary, for whatever reasons, the tribesman becomes increasingly less of a tribesman and more of a peasant. The process is neither immediate nor is it necessarily absolute, but to the degree that a tribesman becomes dependent, he becomes less of a tribesman.[5]

To a great extent, the process by which people lost their freedom in Europe was economic in nature. The medieval castles were military forts and functioned as kinds of storehouses, but they also developed into trade centers and eventually towns. In the early stages of feudalism, the agricultural worker "traded" his freedom for security from military aggression. But increasingly, over the centuries, a primary function of the medieval town became that of the marketplace.

"It is the market, in one form or another, that pulls out from the compact social relations of self-contained primitive communities some parts of men's doings and puts people into fields of economic activity that are increasingly independent of the rest of what goes on in local life. The local traditional and moral world and the wider and more impersonal world of the market are in principle distinct, and opposed to each other. . . ."[6]

The European "discovery" of North America led to the transposition of European medieval law and customs to the Americas. To be sure, Spanish medieval law differed in some respects from that of France, and both differed in some respects from that of England, but an understanding of Medieval Europe is essential to an analysis of European-Haudenosaunee legal history and also to any analysis of the process of colonialism. Medieval Europe is the period of the rise of growing centralization and consolidation of power by the ruling kinships (kings) over vast territories that are specific to the North American experience. It is also the period of the rise and growth of European cities as centers of trade and sources of political power. The European laws of nations, as they were applied to the Americas, were medieval laws.

"Europeans used a great variety of means to attain mastery, of which armed combat was only one. Five principles were available to a European sovereignty for laying claim to legitimate jurisdiction over an American territory and its people: papal donation, first discovery, sustained possession,

voluntary self-subjugation by the natives, and armed conquest successfully maintained. The colony was the means of translating a formal claim to the effective actuality of government, and it was "colonial" in both senses of that ambiguous word. The huddled villages of Europeans were colonies in the sense of being offshoots or reproductions of their parent societies, and these villages exerted power over larger native populations in the sense more clearly implied by the word colonialism."[7]

The European invaders, from the first, attempted to claim Indians as their subjects. Where the Indian people resisted, as in the case of the Haudenosaunee, the Europeans rationalized that resistance to be an incapacity for civilization. The incapacity for civilization rationale became the basis for the phenomenon in the West that is known today as racism.

The Europeans landed on the shores of the Americas and immediately claimed the territories for their sovereign. They then attempted, especially in the case of France and Spain, to make peasants of the Indians. The English, who had already experimented with the enclosure system and who thus colonized North America with landless peasants who were driven by a desperation rooted in their own history, at first simply drove the Indians off the land by force.

The European legal systems had, and apparently have developed, no machinery to recognize the rights of peoples, other than dictators or sovereigns, to land. When the Europeans came to North America, they attempted to simply make vassals of the Native leaders. When that failed, they resorted to other means. The essential thrust of European powers has been an attempt to convert ". . . the Indian person from membership in an unassimilable caste to membership in a social class integrated into Euro-American institutions."[8]

The dispossession of the Native people was accomplished by the Europeans in the bloodiest and most brutal chapter of human history. They were acts committed, seemingly, by a people without conscience or standards of behavior. To this day, the United States and Canada deny the existence of the lawful governments of the Haudenosaunee and other Native nations, a continuation of the policy of genocide that has marked the process known as colonialism. In the face of overwhelming evidence to the contrary, both governments and the governments of Latin America deny the commission of genocide, either physical or cultural.

Their reasoning is patently medieval and racist: ". . . Civilization is that quality possessed by people with civil governments, civil government is Europe's kind of government; Indians did not have Europe's kind of government, therefore Indians were not civilized. Uncivilized people live in wild anarchy; therefore Indians did not have government at all. And THERE-FORE Europeans could not have been doing anything wrong—were in fact performing a noble mission—by bringing government and civilization to the poor savages."9 Today, as in medieval times, the Indo-European government follows a "might makes right" policy. Colonialism is a process often misunderstood and misinterpreted. It is a policy that has long survived the medieval period in which it was born. Many Western institutions are in fact colonial institutions of Western culture. The churches, for example, operate in virtually the same manner as did the feudal lords. First, they identify a people whose loyalty they wish to secure in an expansionist effort. Then they charter a group to conduct a "mission." If that group is successful, they become, in effect, the spiritual sovereigns or dictators of those whose loyalty they command. That process in organized Christianity may actually be more ancient than the process of political colonialism described here.

Modern multinational corporations operate in much the same way. They identify a market or an area that has the resources they want. They then obtain a charter, or some form of sanction from a Western government, and they send what amounts to a colonizing force into the area. If they successfully penetrate the area, that area becomes a sort of economic colony of the multinational. The greatest resistance to that form of penetration has been mounted by local nationalists.

In North America, educational institutions operate under the same colonial process. Schools are chartered by a sovereign (such as the state, or the Bureau of Indian Affairs) to penetrate the Native community. The purpose in doing so is to integrate the Native people into society as workers and consumers, the Industrial Society's version of peasants. The sovereign recognizes, and practically allows, no other form of socializing institution for the young. As in the days of the medieval castle, the sovereign demands absolute fealty. Under this peculiar legal system, the Western sovereign denies the existence of those whose allegiance he cannot obtain. Some become, by this rationale, illegitimate.

This concept of illegitimacy is then interpreted into official government policy. In the United States, the colonizer has created two categories of Native peoples: federally recognized and nonfederally recognized. In more recent years, the government has taken to a policy of nonrecognition of an entity entitled "Urban Indians." In Canada there exist four legal definitions of Native people. They are divided into "status," "non-status," "metis," and "enfranchised." Both countries carry on the policy of consistently referring to "Indians and Eskimos," as though Eskimos were separate and not a Native people of the Western Hemisphere.

Chiefs of the Six Nation Iroquois Conferderacy at the inauguration ceremony of the United Nations headquarters, New York City, October 24, 1949. Left to right: David Hill, Clinton Rickard, Harry Patterson, Angus Horne, Thomas Beauvais, and Lone Wolf.

UN/DPI Photo

The United States and Canada practice blatant colonialism in the areas affecting political institutions of the Native peoples. In 1924, Canada's new Indian Act[10] established the legal sanction for the imposition of neocolonial "elective system" governments within the Native peoples' territories. In the United States, the same goal was accomplished with the passage of the 1934 Indian Reorganization Act (IRA).[11] Both pieces of legislation provided compulsive, chartered, political colonies among Native peoples. These "elective systems" owe their existence and fealty to the United States and Canada, and not to the Native peoples. They are, by definition, colonies that create classes of political peasants. They are governments only to the degree an external social caste allows them to be governments. They are, in most places in Native peoples' territories, the only forms of government recognized by the colonizers.

The Haudenosaunee have also been subjected to the many forms of colonialism of the Western governments. Our first contact with a Western people came in 1609 when a French military expedition under Samuel de Champlain murdered some Mohawk people along the lake that now bears his name. Later, when the Dutch came, the first treaty (or agreement) that we made with a European power was the Two Row Treaty[12] in which we clarified our position—that we are a distinct, free, and sovereign people. The Dutch accepted that agreement.

But the European nations have never honored the agreement. Many times France attempted to dominate the Haudenosaunee through conquest. England often used every means possible, including coercion, threats, and military force, to extend her sovereignty over us. Each time we resisted.

The United States entered into solemn treaties with the Haudenosaunee, and each time has ignored virtually each and every provision of the treaties that guarantee our rights as a separate nation. Only the sections of the treaties that refer to land cessions, sections that often were fraudulently obtained, have validity in the eyes of the United States courts or governments.

The mechanism for the colonization of the Haudenosaunee territory is found in legal fiction in the United States Constitution. That document purports to give Congress power to "regulate commerce with foreign nations and among the several States, and with Indian tribes."[13] Contrary to every principle of international law, Congress has expanded that section to an assertion of "plenary" power, a doctrine that asserts absolute authority over our territories.[14] This assertion has been repeatedly urged upon our people, although we have never agreed to that relationship and we have never been conquered in warfare. The Haudenosaunee are vassals to no people—we are a free nation, and we have never surrendered our rights as a free people.

From the beginning of its existence, the United States has conducted a reign of terror in the Haudenosaunee territory. Colonial agents entered our country between 1784 and 1842 and returned to Washington with treaties for cessions of land fraudulently obtained with persons not authorized to make land transfers. The Haudenosaunee Council, which is the only legitimate body authorized to conduct land transactions, never signed any agreements surrendering the territories.

The United States occupied the lands under threats of war, although there were no acts that justified war measures. When the Haudenosaunee gathered evidence to prove that the treaties were fraudulent and therefore illegal under any interpretation of law, the United States courts countered by inventing the Political Question Doctrine.[15] This doctrine basically asserts that Congress cannot commit fraud and that the courts cannot question Congress' political judgment, although the United States courts find congressional acts in other areas of the law to be unconstitutional regularly.

Because the Haudenosaunee refused to sell the land, the United States simply refused to recognize our government. Instead, they recognized those colonized individuals who would agree to sell the land and whose loyalties lie with Washington. In 1848, the United States simply recognized an "elective system" on the Seneca Nation lands,[16] creating a colonial government on the largest of our remaining territories in what is called by the colonizers "New York State."

There followed a long list of moves by the United States to exterminate the Haudenosaunee. There were treaties that entirely dispossessed, for all practical purposes, the Cayuga and Oneida Nations in their ancestral lands.[17] There were treaties, such as the Treaty of 1797,[18] which recognized the sale by individuals of the territory of the Kanienkehaka, an area of nine million acres of land exchanged for the sum of one thousand dollars. There were attempts from 1821 to 1842 to remove the Haudenosaunee from the territories called "New York" by the colonists to other areas now called Wisconsin and Kansas.[19] These efforts resulted in the displacement of some of our people to those areas. In 1851, there was an attempt to evict the Seneca people from their lands at Tonawanda.

In 1886, there was an attempt to divide the Haudenosaunee lands into severalty under the Dawes Act,[20] an attempt that was not entirely successful. In 1924, the United States passed The Indian Citizenship Act (ICA), which attempted to give United States citizenship to all Native people.[21] The Haudenosaunee strongly rejected the concept that we could ever be United States citizens. But the feudal laws of the colonizers have been relentless.

Also in 1924, Canada militarily invaded our territories on the Grand River and forcibly installed a colonial government there.[22] The episode was repeated by Canada in 1934 on our territories at the Thames River community of Oneida.[23]

In 1948 and 1950, Congress passed laws giving civil and criminal jurisdiction to New York State,[24] although Congress was never given such jurisdiction by the Haudenosaunee. In 1964, Congress passed Public Law 88-533, the Kinzua Dam Act,[25] which resulted in the flooding of almost all of the habitable lands of the Seneca at Alleghany, and virtually destroyed the Native communities and culture there. That act also provided for the termination of the Seneca Nation, a process that would have ended even the colonial government there, and which would have moved the denial of our existence a little closer to reality.

In addition to these legal kinds of colonization, the Haudenosaunee have been subjected to every other kind of colonization imaginable. Churches, school systems, and every form of Western penetration have made political, economic, and cultural peasants of some of our populations. The continuing denial of our political existence has been accomplished by an almost overwhelming psychological, economic, and spiritual attack by the colonial institutions of the West.

For over three hundred years, our people have been under a virtual state of siege. During this entire time we have never once given up our struggle. Our strategies have, of necessity, changed. But the will and determination to continue on remains the same. Throughout these years, European historians have recorded the position of the Haudenosaunee.

During the 1920s, one of our leaders, a man named Deskaheh, came to this city to seek help for his people.[26] At that time, the international body that existed did not truly represent the world community. Many cultures and nations were not recognized. Now, years later, we have returned, and our message remains the same.

Our elders have watched the rebirth of this international institution. In 1949, a delegation of the Haudenosaunee attended the foundation ceremony for the United Nations building in New York City.[27] In 1972, our people journeyed to Sweden to take part in an international conference on the environment and ecology.[28] All through these times we have taken notice of the changes that have occurred within this institution.

Now we find ourselves in Geneva, Switzerland, once again. For those of us present, and the many at home, we have assumed the duty of carrying on our peoples' struggle. Invested in the names we carry today are the lives of thousands of generations of both the past and the future. On their behalf, also, we ask that the Non-Governmental Organizations join us in our struggle to obtain our full rights and protection under the rules of international law and the World Community.

Policies of Oppression in the Name of "Democracy"

Economic History of the Haudenosaunee

The Haudenosaunee, People of the Longhouse, who are known to many Europeans as the Six Nations Iroquois, have inhabited their territories since time immemorial. During the time prior to the coming of the Europeans, it is said that ours were a happy and prosperous people. Our lands provided abundantly for our needs. Our people lived long, healthy, and productive lives. Before the Europeans came, we were an affluent people, rich in the gifts of our country. We were a strong people in both our minds and bodies. Throughout most of that time, we lived in peace.

Prior to the arrival of the colonists, we were a people who lived by hunting and gathering, and practiced a form of agriculture that was not labor intensive. The economy of the people was an extremely healthful Way of Life, and our peoples were very healthy—among the finest athletes in the world. There were some, in those times, who lived to be one hundred twenty years and more, and our runners were unexcelled for speed and endurance.

Among our people we refer to our culture as "Ongwe Honwekah." This refers to a Way of Life that is peculiar to the Haudenosaunee. It is virtually impossible for us to recount, specifically, the history of "Haudenosaunee economics." As will become evident, our economy, that way in which our people manage their resources and the relationship of that management to the total organization of our society, are processes completely bound together. The distribution of goods, in our traditional society, was accomplished through institutions that are not readily identified as economic institutions by other societies. The Haudenosaunee do not have specific economic institutions, nor do we have specifically distinct political institutions. Rather, what European people identify as institutions of one classification or another serve many different purposes among the Haudenosaunee.

We were a people of a great forest. That forest was a source of great wealth. It was a place in which was to be found huge hardwoods and an almost unimaginable abundance and variety of nuts, berries, roots, and herbs. In addition to these, the rivers teemed with fish and the forest and its meadows abounded with game. It was, in fact, a kind of Utopia, a place where no one went hungry, a place where the people were happy and healthy.

Our traditions were such that we were careful not to allow our populations to rise to numbers that would overtax the other forms of life. We practiced strict forms of conservation. Our culture is based on a principle that directs us to constantly think about the welfare of seven generations into the future. Our belief in this principle acts as a restraint to the development of practices that would cause suffering in the future. To this end, our people took only as many animals as were needed to meet our needs. Not until the arrival of the colonists did the wholesale slaughter of animals occur.

We feel that many people will be confused when we say that ours is a Way of Life, and that our economy cannot be separated from the many aspects of our culture. Our economy is unlike that of Western peoples. We believe that all things in the world were created by what the English language forces us to call "Spiritual Beings," including one that we call the Great Creator. All things in this world belong to the Creator and the spirits of the world. We also believe that we are required to honor these beings, in respect of the gift of life.

In accordance with our ways, we are required to hold many kinds of feasts and ceremonies that can best be described as "giveaways." It is said that among our people, our leaders, those whom the Anglo people insist on calling "chiefs," are the poorest of us. By the laws of our culture, our leaders are both political and spiritual leaders. They are leaders of many ceremonies that require the distribution of great wealth. As spiritual and political leaders, they provide a kind of economic conduit. To become a political leader, a person is required to be a spiritual leader; and to become a spiritual leader, a person must be extraordinarily generous in terms of material goods.

Our leaders, in fact, are leaders of categories of large extended families. Those large extended families function as economic units in a Way of Life that has as its base the Domestic Mode of Production. Before the colonists came, we had our own means of production and distribution adequate to meet all the peoples' needs. We would have been unable to exist as nations were it not so.

Our basic economic unit is the family. The means of distribution, aside from simple trade, consists of a kind of spiritual tradition manifested in the functions of the religious/civic leaders in a highly complex religious, governmental, and social structure.

The Haudenosaunee have no concept of private property. This concept would be a contradiction to a people who believe that the Earth belongs to the Creator. Property is an idea by which people can be excluded from having access to lands or other means of producing a livelihood. That idea would destroy our culture, which requires that every individual live in service to the Spiritual Ways and The People. That idea (property) would produce slavery. The acceptance of the idea of property would produce leaders whose functions would favor excluding people from access to property, and they would cease to perform their functions as leaders of our societies and distributors of goods.

Before the colonists came, we had no consciousness about a concept of commodities. Everything, even the things we make, belong to the Creators of Life and are to be returned ceremonially, and in reality, to the owners. Our people live a simple life, one unencumbered by the need for endless material commodities. The fact that their needs are few means that all the peoples' needs are easily met. It is also true that our means of distribution is an eminently fair process, one in which all of the people share in all the material wealth all of the time.

Our Domestic Mode of Production has a number of definitions that are culturally specific. Our peoples' economy requires a community of people and is not intended to define an economy based on the self-sufficient nuclear family. Some modern economists estimate that in most parts of the world the isolated nuclear family cannot produce enough to survive in a Domestic Mode of Production. In any case, that particular mode of subsistence, by our cultural definition, is not an economy at all.

Ours was a wealthy society. No one suffered from want. All had the right to food, clothing, and shelter. All shared in the bounty of the spiritual ceremonies and the Natural World. No one stood in any material relationship of power over anyone else. No one could deny anyone access to the things they needed. All in all, before the colonists came, ours was a beautiful and rewarding Way of Life.

The colonists arrived with many institutions and strategies designed to destroy the Way of Life of the People of the Longhouse. In 1609, Samuel de Champlain led a French military expedition that attacked a part of the Mohawk people on the lake now named "Lake Champlain." Champlain arrived in search of wealth and was specifically interested in generating some kind of trade in beaver pelts with the Algonquin people of the area. He demonstrated his firearms to them, letting them see, for the first time, the power of guns.

Champlain, accompanied by his newly found business partners, marched into the center of Mohawk territory. This war party encountered about two hundred Mohawks. The first volley of gunfire killed three men, and the second created such confusion that the Mohawks retreated, leaving twelve men who were taken captive.

The period of warfare that followed this incident has come to be known as the "Beaver Wars." The introduction of trade in beaver pelts inevitably triggered a long series of colonial wars. It represented the escalation of disputes among neighbors into a full-scale struggle for survival in the forests of the Native people of North America.

The European penetration affected every facet of the Native Way of Life from the very moment of contact. The natural economies, cultures, politics, and military affairs became totally altered. Nations learned that to be without firearms meant physical annihilation. To be without access to beaver pelts meant no means to buy firearms.

The trade in beaver pelts, and the now necessary weaponry, introduced factors never before encountered by the Native people. Trade meant that long routes over which goods were to be transported had to be secured. The only way that was possible was for the entire area to be in friendly hands. Any potential disruptor of the trade routes must either be pacified or eliminated.

With the introduction of firearms, war became a deadly business. It was made more deadly because the European strategy of economic penetration was to stimulate warfare among the Native nations to determine which would have the goods for trade. Out of necessity, to protect themselves from annihilation, the People of the Longhouse entered the beaver trade. The pelts were used to buy more firearms and goods that made it possible for more men to trap more beaver more efficiently. The marketplaces of France, Holland, and England were eager for the "New World" merchandise.

Shortly after the encounter on Lake Champlain, the Haudenosaunee began trading with Holland, which had established posts along the Hudson River. A large part of the trade involved firearms. French historians recount that the People of the Longhouse were very skillful at the strategies of battle, and within a short time the Algonquin people were defeated. Their defeat was aided by the fact that the French had not taken seriously their pledges of aid to the Algonquin.

So intense became the need for European goods, especially firearms, that by 1640 the beaver were becoming scarce in the Haudenosaunee territories. Pressure from the newly created European frontiers was steadily increasing. Warfare was also common between the various colonizers. The Haudenosaunee were well aware of what was occurring to the east. The Dutch, shortly after their arrival, began a series of genocidal wars that ended in the utter annihilation of the Native peoples of the Lower Hudson River Valley. In New England, the Pequot Nation was nearly obliterated by the Puritan and English colonists there.

Knowledge of these massacres greatly influenced Haudenosaunee defense policy. To the east were the Dutch and English, whose presence was necessary as a source of firearms. Yet, they represented a constant potential of movement of their frontiers westward into the Longhouse. To the north was the colony of France, which was supplying arms to the western Native nations. France also threatened to gain a monopoly over the beaver trade, which was increasingly centered to the north and west of Lake Erie and Lake Ontario.

France made repeated attempts to send missionaries, especially Jesuits, among the nations of the Haudenosaunee. These missions were the major tool of propaganda for the European nations. Missionaries then, as today, were expected to carry more than the message of Christianity. They served as lay ambassadors of their culture, splitting off individuals from families, families from villages, and villages from nations, one by one. Some priests even served as the leaders of troops going into battle.

The missionaries made persistent attacks on the economic structures of the People of the Longhouse. They specifically attacked the spiritual ceremonies as "pagan," and thereby sought to end the practice of giveaways and public feasts. In addition, they sought to break the power of the clans by causing a division that would split the people into nuclear households.

Europeans' churches, especially in colonial practice, take on their feudal roles as economic institutions. Among Natural World people, they are the most dangerous agents of destruction. They invariably seek to destroy the spiritual/economic bonds of the people to the forests, land, and animals. They spread both ideologies and technologies that make people slaves to the extractive system that defines colonialism.

In 1704, the first Anglican missionaries were sent by England to the Mohawks living along the Mohawk River. In 1710, a delegation of Mohawk chiefs received an invitation to visit England. They returned bearing four bibles, a prayer book, and a communion plate for the Anglican chapel, gifts from Queen Anne. But the missionaries also brought behind them a long, long tail. To house themselves they needed a mission, to protect the mission they needed a fort, and to propagate the faith, they needed a school. Missionaries spread more than the word of God. The British Empire was fast entering the Haudenosaunee territories, and there was more to come.

The warlike European kingdoms were constantly fighting among themselves. There were three wars during the eighteenth century just between France and England: Queen Anne's War (1701 to 1713), King George's War (1744 to 1748), and the French and Indian War, known to the European world as the War of the Spanish Succession (1754 to 1763). It is clear from the records of the time that the People of the Longhouse remained neutral throughout these conflicts, although individuals on the road to assimilation, such as the Anglicized Mohawks who had been coerced into roles as British peasants, could be counted on to aid the colonizers.

If France was unsuccessful in her attempts at military penetration of the territory of the Longhouse, England was far more successful in her social and religious colonization of the eastern part of our territories. William Johnson was an Irish immigrant who became famous for his influence over certain Mohawks. As an agent of the British Crown, he maintained an embassy as an operation base close to the Mohawk country. He took several Native women as concubines and had several children by them, none of whom he ever recognized as his heirs. His position was known as "British Superintendent of Indian Affairs for the Northern Department." He is widely credited, by European historians, as a successful manipulator of events and developments on the frontier during his tenure. In today's context, Johnson would be working as an ambassador to a Third World country, executing simultaneously diplomatic, military, intelligence, and foreign aid operations.

During his tenure, he engineered the establishment of a beachhead from which immigrants could move westward to broaden the colony. Mohawk lands along the Susquehanna and Mohawk Rivers were increasingly encroached upon by the British settlers, including Johnson himself. By the spring of 1765, the carefully managed Longhouse environment was in trouble, as ignorant and destructive peasant settlers almost eradicated the deer herds.

There was so much trouble with the peasant settlers that the Mohawks, who had so generously allowed them to share their lands, were actually

considering moving westward into Oneida territories to gain some peace. By the spring of 1765, many Mohawks had already been displaced and were living as refugees among the other nation.

William Johnson was a master public relations man for the King. He would, on the one hand, apologize for the behavior of the frontiersmen and urge the Mohawks to be patient, and on the other hand encourage more settlers to move into the Mohawk lands. He would make a great show of protecting Haudenosaunee interests, and in that way encourage the People of the Longhouse to seek a resolution at the bargaining table, where they invariably ended up trading land to gain a temporary peace.

Throughout this period, many other Native peoples had been moving into our territories to gain some respite from the colonial onslaught. Far to the south, in the colonized area known as the Carolinas, the Tuscarora were faced with imminent destruction. In their drive to gain some more land and economic advantage, English colonizers were using the same techniques that were being employed in the northeast. In 1713, the dispossessed Tuscaroras withdrew from their homelands and sought protection in the territories of the Haudenosaunee. They were not the only people who were displaced. Delawares, Tuteloes, Shawnees, and others fled to the Haudenosaunee lands seeking peace.

Peace, however, was not to be. At the approach of the American Revolution, the Haudenosaunee did everything possible to remain neutral. With the decline of France, and the increasing decline in the importance of trade, the settler bourgeoisie of the Anglo colonies cast an increasingly envious eye on the lands of the Longhouse. Still, our military power was formidable, and our resolve was to remain neutral.

The policy of England, however, was to involve the Haudenosaunee in the war. To accomplish this goal, they resorted to bribery, trickery, false propaganda, and emotional appeal. The Haudenosaunee continued its policy of neutrality throughout. Both the colonists and the "loyalists" entered our territories in search of mercenaries. The loyalist strategy was the more successful. They were able to draw some of our people into a battle with the revolting colonists.

The Treaty of Paris in 1783, which ended the war, made no provision, at least in writing, for the Native nations that the British Crown had solemnly promised to protect. Thus the representatives of the People of the Longhouse held an international treaty meeting with the new federation, called the United States of America, in September of 1784. The U.S. demanded huge cessions of territory, especially from the Senecas. The warriors who had been delegated to the meeting eventually signed the treaty.[1] However, they had not been authorized to commit the Haudenosaunee without consulting them.[2] For a time, the terms of the treaty were not known, as the U.S. would not provide the Haudenosaunee with a copy of the document. As many Native people know, to their regret, signing a treaty and the ratification of a treaty are two separate acts, each necessary before a treaty becomes valid. Although the U.S. Congress ratified the treaty, the legislative council of the Haudenosaunee met at Buffalo Creek and renounced the agreement.[3]

Somehow the United States takes the position that the Haudenosaunee ceased to exist by the year 1784, although the Longhouse has continued to this day. There is ample evidence that all the nations continued to participate in the matters of the Great Council, the legislative body of the Confederacy. None of the nations of the League has ever declared themselves separate from the Confederation. The Oneidas, whose reputed allegiance to the United States was based on the existence of Oneida mercenaries, continued to send their delegates to the Council, and the Tuscarora remain firmly attached to the League. The Onondagas, Senecas, Cayugas, and Mohawks continue to hold their positions within the League. Although the Haudenosaunee have been severely disrupted by the westward expansion of the United States, the subsequent surrounding of their lands, and the attempts to devour its people, the Six Nations Confederacy continues to function. Indeed, today its strength continues to be increasing.

By pretending that the Haudenosaunee government no longer exists, both the U.S. and Britain illegally took Haudenosaunee territories by simply saying the territories belong to them. To this day, Canada, the former colony of England, has never made a treaty for the lands in the St. Lawrence River Valley. But the truth continues to remain and plague officials yet today. The Haudenosaunee territories are not and have never been part of the U.S. or Canada. The citizens of the Haudenosaunee are a separate people, distinct from either Canada or the United States. Because of this, the Haudenosaunee refuse to recognize a border drawn by a foreign people through our lands.

The policy of the dispossession of North American Native peoples, first by the European kingdoms, and later by the settler regimes, began with the first contact. Dispossession took a number of approaches: the so-called "just warfare" was a strategy by which Native nations were deemed to have offended the Crown and their elimination by fire and sword was justified. That was followed by the Treaty Period in which Native nations were "induced" to sell their lands and move westward. The Treaty Period was in full swing at the beginning of the nineteenth century. By 1815, the governor of New York was agitating for the removal of all Native people from the state for "their own good."[4]

While the infamous Trail of Tears was removing Native peoples from the southeast to Oklahoma, New York State was lobbying for a treaty in 1838[5] that was intended to remove the Haudenosaunee, who were on lands that the state wanted, away to an area of Kansas. The principal victims were to be the Senecas.[6]

Like the Termination Policy[7] a century later, the Removal Policy was eventually abandoned due in part to the bad press received during the Cherokee removal in 1838. During the process of the Cherokee removal, thousands of Cherokee men, women, children, and elders were subjected to conditions that caused them to die of exposure, starvation, and neglect.[8]

In 1871, the U.S. Congress passed an act that included a clause that treaties would no longer be made with "Indian Nations."[9] It was at this time that official United States policy toward Native people began to shift to a new strategy. Reports to Congress began to urge that the Native people be assimilated into U.S. society as quickly as possible. The policy of fire and sword simply began to become less popular among an increasingly significant percentage of the United States population. The principal hindrance to the assimilation of the Native people, according to its most vocal adherents, was the Indian land base. The Native land base was held in common, and this was perceived as an uncivilized and un-American practice. The assimilationists urged that if every Indian family owned its own farmstead, they could more readily acquire "civilized" traits. Thus the Dawes Act of 1887[10] ordered the Native nations stripped of their land base, resulting in the transfer of millions of acres to European hands.[11]

There was consistent pressure in the New York legislature to "civilize" the Haudenosaunee. To accomplish this, all vestiges of Haudenosaunee nationality needed to be destroyed. This is the nineteenth century origin of the policy to "educate" the Indian to be culturally European.[12] It was thought that when the Indian was successfully Europeanized, he would no longer be distinct and separate, and that there would no longer be an Indigenous people with their own customs and economy. At that point, the Indian could simply be declared to have assimilated into the United States or Canadian society The net effect would dispense with the entire concept of Native nations, and that would extinguish the claims of those nations to their lands. The report of the Whipple Committee to the New York legislature in 1888[13] was clear: "Exterminate the Tribe."

In 1924, the Canadian government "abolished" Haudenosaunee government at the Grand River territory. The Oneida and Akwesasne territories were invaded and occupied by Canadian troops in order to establish neocolonial "elective systems" in the name of democracy. Also in 1924, the United States government passed legislation declaring all American Indians to be United States citizens.[14] The 1924 Citizenship Act was an attempt to deny the existence of Native nations and the rights of these Native nations to their lands. The denial of the existence of Native nations is a way of legitimizing the colonists' claims to the lands.

This concept is furthered by the imposition of non-Native forms of government. This also serves to fulfill the colonizer's need to destroy any semblance of sovereignty. The actual process for taking lands can be accomplished when the Native nation no longer exists in its original context—when it is less of a nation.

With all semblance of a Native nation's original context destroyed, Canada and the United States can rationalize that integration has occurred. With this rationale in hand, both governments have set out to enact their final solutions to the "Indian Problem."

The Haudenosaunee vigorously objected to the Citizenship Act and maintains to this day that the People of the Longhouse are not citizens

A Haudenosaunee delegate to Geneva, Aaron Oaks, Akwesasne Mohawk.

of Canada or the United States, but are citizens of their own nations of the League.

The Termination Acts of the 1950s were efforts to simply declare that the Native nations no longer exist and to appropriate their lands.[15] The acts were so disastrous that they caused something of a national scandal. "St. Regis," the European name for Akwesasne, was one of our territories targeted by the Bureau of Indian Affairs (BIA) as "ready for integration."

The BIA based its recommendation on the fact that many Mohawks had acquired at least some of the material conditions that made their community outwardly indistinguishable from the white communities. In fact, however, Akwesasne was, and is, very different from the small towns in the area surrounding it.

Termination submerged as an official policy in the late 1960s. But termination is simply a means to an end. The objective is the economic exploitation of a people and their lands. The taking of lands and the denial and destruction of Native nations are concrete and undeniable elements in

113

the colonization process as it is applied to Native people surrounded by a settler state.

Tools to accomplish this end include guns, disease, revised histories, repressive missionaries, and indoctrinating teachers, and these things are often cloaked in codes of law. In the twentieth century, the taking of the land and the destruction of the culture and Native economy serve to force Native people into roles as industrial workers, just as in the nineteenth century the same processes forced Native people in the U.S. and Canada into roles as landless peasants.

The Haudenosaunee has, over a period of 375 years, met every definition of an oppressed nation. It has been subjected to raids of extermination from France, England, and the United States. Its people have been driven from their lands, impoverished, and persecuted for their Haudenosaunee customs. It has been the victim of fraudulent dealings from three European governments that have openly expressed the goal of the extermination of the Haudenosaunee. Our children have been taught to despise their ancestors, their culture, their religion, and their traditional economy. Recently, it has been a government-sponsored fad to have bilingual/bicultural programs in the schools. These programs are not a sincere effort to revitalize the Haudenosaunee; they exist as an integrationists' ploy to imply "acceptance" from the dominating culture.

Revisionist United States and British historians have cloaked the past in a veil of lies. The national and local governments of the Haudenosaunee have been suppressed and usurped by the colonial authorities and their neo-colonial Indian helpers to carry out policies of repression in the name of "democracy." Generation after generation has seen the Haudenosaunee land base, and therefore its economic base, shrink under the expansionist policies of the United States, Great Britain, and Canada.

The world is told by colonial government propaganda machines that the Haudenosaunee are simply "victims of civilization and progress." The truth is that they are the victims of a conscious and persistent effort of destruction directed at them by the European governments and their heirs in North America. The Haudenosaunee is not suffering a terminal illness of natural causes—it is being deliberately strangled to death by those who would benefit from its death.

Although treaties may often have been bad deals for the Native nations, the United States and Canada chose not to honor those that exist because to do so would require the return of much of the economic base and sovereignty to the Haudenosaunee. The treaties contain the potential for independent survival of the Native people. The dishonoring of treaties

114

is essential to the goal of the U.S. and Canadian vested interests that are organized to remove any and all obstacles to their exploitation of the Earth and her peoples.

The European nations of the Western Hemisphere continue to wage war against the Haudenosaunee. The weapons have changed somewhat—Indian education programs and social workers, neocolonial Indian officials, and racist laws are used first. If these methods fail, the guns are still ready, as recent history at Akwesasne and South Dakota have shown.

The effect of all these policies has been the destruction of the culture and therefore the economy of the People of the Longhouse. The traditional economy has been largely replaced by the colonial economy, which serves multinational corporate interests. The colonial economy is one that extracts labor and materials from the people of the Haudenosaunee for the benefit of the colonizers. The Christian religions, the school systems, and the neocolonial elective systems all work towards these goals.

We are an economically poor people today. Few of us can afford to support the spiritual ceremonies that form the foundations of our traditional economies. The money economy is not adaptable to the real economy of our people. Few of our peoples participate in the Domestic Mode of Production that defines the traditional economy. This is largely because the colonizer's education system, and also more systematic and brutal attempts at acculturation, have placed neocolonial governments on our territories. On some of the Haudenosaunee lands, the Canadian and United States governments' moneys employ one-third of all employable workers, creating an economic dependence among potential leadership of the Haudenosaunee and actively recruiting people away from the Domestic Mode of Production. The traditional economy is under heavy attack from many directions, and all else is an economy of exploitation. The political oppression, the social oppression, the economic oppression, all have the same face. These are the tools of genocide in North America.

Genocide is alive and well in the territory of the Haudenosaunee. Its technicians are in Washington, Ottawa, and Albany, and its agents control the schools, the churches, and the neocolonial "elective system" offices found in our territories. The oppression of the Haudenosaunee has taken its toll—but the Haudenosaunee continues to meet in Council, and its members are on the rise. The Haudenosaunee, the People of the Longhouse, still have a long history ahead. We have developed strategies to resist the economic effects of the conditions we face. But, those strategies require that we revitalize our social and political institutions. This can only be accomplished on sufficient lands within the ancient boundaries of our territories.

We are living in a period of time during which we expect to see great changes in the economy of the colonizers. The imperial powers of the world appear to be facing successful resistance to expansion in Africa, Asia, and other parts of the world. We will soon see the end of an economy based on the supply of cheap oil, natural gas, and other resources, and that will greatly change the face of the world.

For the moment, there is more wealth, more goods and services, more automation than has ever existed in the history of mankind. The world is living in an age of manufactured affluence. But the people of the world have rarely been told the costs in terms of people's lives and the suffering that this affluence has extracted from each of us. Even the people in North America, who seemingly benefit from all these "advances," seem to be unaware of the destruction they are experiencing. The "Modern Age" and its consumer values have altered, in very basic ways, the very structure of human society and the basic conditions of the Natural World.

The modern family is an institution that is presently under a great deal of stress. The family in Western society has undergone great changes over the last century. As the Westernization of the world continues, all peoples will be faced with similar stresses and turmoils.

We, the Haudenosaunee, have clear choices about the future. One of the choices which we have faced is whether to become Westernized, or to remain true to the Way of Life our forefathers developed for us. We have stated our understanding of the history of the changes that have created the present conditions. We have chosen to remain Haudenosaunee, and within the context of our Way of Life, to set a course of liberation for ourselves and the future generations.

Our liberation process is not one that is exclusive to us as humans, but also includes the other life forms that coexist and are as oppressed as we. The liberation of the Natural World is a process that is being undertaken in a most difficult environment. The people surrounding us seem to be intent on destroying themselves and every living thing.

Throughout the past four hundred years, the Haudenosaunee have exerted a great influence on the lives of millions of people. Theories about democracy and a classless society have been developed from inadequate interpretations of the true nature of those ideals. This conference may be the time that begins a process that moves toward more real definitions of these concepts.

In our homelands, our people are still struggling and developing strategies for survival. In the Mohawk country, our people have reoccupied lands for the purpose of revitalizing our culture and economy. This settlement, known as Kanién:ke, has been successfully held for more than three years.[16]

The Oneida people have been waging a court battle for several years to regain 265,000 acres illegally taken in the 1700s.[17] The Cayugas have also been engaged in an effort to regain 100,000 acres taken during the same period as the theft from the Oneidas.[18] The Onondagas and Tuscaroras have been carrying on an unceasing battle to gain control of the education that their children receive. The Senecas have been forced into a long struggle to protect the last pieces of their land still under traditional government, the lands at the Tonawanda territory. Every day of our lives finds us defending ourselves from some form of intrusion by the state of New York or the United States or Canadian governments.

If we are to continue to survive, we need the help of the international community. We need an external presence to bring some sort of stability to the situation of our people. We have learned, too frequently, that what is good law today can rapidly be changed into bad law. Both Canada and the United States have taught us that their legal systems are part of the political machinery that effects the oppression of our peoples.

We are nations by every definition of the term. We have been unable to obtain any semblance of justice in the court systems of the United States or Canada, and we suffer horrible legal injustices that have terrible economic and social consequences for our people. Many of our legal problems involve land and sovereignty over land, and land is the basis of our economy. We are seeking our rights in those areas under international law.

Lastly, we require economic assistance in the forms of economic aid and technical assistance. We are aware that there exist various international figures who have technical expertise and who are conscious of development in the context of specific cultures. Our case is appropriate to the deliberations of the United Nations Decolonization Committee.[19] We are engaged in a struggle to decolonize our lands and our lives, but we cannot accomplish this goal alone and unaided.

For centuries we have known that each individual's action creates conditions and situations that affect the world. For centuries we have been careful to avoid any action unless it carried a long-range prospect of promoting harmony and peace in the world. In that context, with our brothers and sisters of the Western Hemisphere, we have journeyed here to discuss these important matters with the other members of the Family of Man.

Our Strategy for Survival

The invasion of the Western Hemisphere by European powers was preceded by centuries of social development that had resulted in societies in which the interests of the few had effectively become national policies, and the interests of the many were without a voice in national affairs. In order that we might formulate a strategy for survival in the modern world, it has been necessary that we look at the forces and processes that threaten survival and begin to understand the real motivations behind those forces. With such an analysis in mind, we may then begin to create viable alternatives and strategies that will enable us to survive in a predictable future.

When history has been presented to us by colonizers, the focal elements have always been political histories. Alexander the Great's armies conquered most of the known ancient word, and when ancient history is studied, Alexander is studied. But are political histories really the correct focus? Does it make any difference in the long run whether Alexander the Great, or Nebuchadnezzar, or Akhnaton, or any other figure in political history ever lived? Other than the effect that Julius Caesar's rise to power had on some individuals in the Roman aristocracy, would history have been any different if some other general had ever dared to cross the Rubicon? Are political histories the correct focus of history in the search for what has affected the lives of billions of the Earth's population?

The really crucial developments in world history have largely been ignored by historians. The most profound changes that have taken place have been in the areas of technological change. Social history has largely been the recounting of the fortunes of the interest groups, which were committed for one reason or another to some form of technological and/or cultural movement. When we are seeking the real cultural revolutions of history, do we not find that the rise of agriculture or animal husbandry or irrigation technology was a thousand times more significant in the history of humankind than were the adventures and political fortunes of the aristocracy and rulers of European countries?

It is important that we who are seeking ways of survival in the twentieth century begin by establishing new definitions and new fields of vision as we try to better understand the past. We need to look to history primarily because the past offers us a laboratory in which we can search to find that inherent process of Western Civilization that paralyzes whole societies and makes them unable to resist the process of colonization. We need to identify the process that so often leads people who are honestly seeking to resist and destroy colonization to unconsciously recreate the elements of their own oppression. And, lastly, we need to understand that within colonization are the exact elements of social organization that are leading the world today to a crisis that promises a foreseeable future of mass starvation, deprivation, and untold hopelessness.

The current crisis that the world is facing is not difficult for people to understand. In the Western Hemisphere, the United States, with six percent of the world's population, uses forty percent of the world's energy resources. The world's supply of fossil fuels is finite, and it is estimated that within thirty years, at the present rate of consumption, the peoples of the world will begin to run out of some of those sources of energy, especially petroleum and natural gas. As the planet begins to run short of cheap energy, it is predictable that the world market economy will suffer and the people of the world who are dependent on that economy will suffer likewise. When the reality of world population growth is placed beside the reality of the current relationship of energy resources and food production, it becomes obvious that worldwide famine is a real possibility.

The spectre of regional famine, or even worldwide famines, cannot be interpreted as the simple product of a world of scarce resources overwhelmed by the needs of expanding human populations. The situation is not that simple. In the United States, for example, a program of energy conservation—insulation of dwellings, offices, and industrial buildings—would cut back energy consumption by more than twenty-five percent in ten years. Even given growth predictions in terms of populations and economy, the U.S. would conceivably enjoy the current standard of living.

The fact is that it is highly unlikely the Unites States will adopt a program of energy conservation that would drastically cut back consumption. The present U.S. political system is controlled by energy interests that are concerned with profit growth, and energy lobbyists are not interested in conservation. In fact, there is no sector of the U.S. economy that will move toward energy conservation as a national energy policy, even though such a policy might conceivably conserve wasted energy that could go toward food production. The problems that we are facing today, as a species that inhabits a planet of limited resources, arise not simply out of physical limitations but from political realities. It is a hard fact of life that the misery that exists in the world will be manipulated in the interests of profit. Politics and economics are intricately linked in the West, and social considerations command inferior priorities in the world's capitals. Energy conservation is not likely to become a policy in the Western countries. The acceptable alternative in the eyes of the multinational energy corporations is the plan to create much more energy through the production of nuclear power plants, especially fast breeder reactors. The predictable misery caused by increases in energy prices that push up food prices (and thus drive the poor from the food marketplace) will also provide the grist for the promotion drives of the multinationals. Nuclear reactors will be made to sound more necessary.

Technologies have political cousins. The same people who own the oil interests have enough clout in many governments to discourage serious and broad-based efforts at energy conservation. They have the ability to command governments to support energy development schemes that will leave them in control of the world's usable energy sources and also in control of the world's marketplace. The same people constitute a class of interest in the Western world that seeks to control every aspect of the economic life of all peoples. Practically every people in the West will be dependent on their technologies for energy and food production, and all who enter the marketplace they control will be colonized.

The roots of a future world that promises misery, poverty, starvation, and chaos lie in the processes that control and destroy the locally specific cultures of the peoples of the world. To the extent that peoples and areas of the world are dependent on the giant multinational corporations that control production, distribution, and consumption patterns, and to that extent only, is the future a dark and ominous one. For this reason, the definition of colonialism needs to be expanded in the consciousness of the peoples of the planet Earth. Colonialism is a process by which Indigenous cultures are subverted and ultimately destroyed in the interests of the worldwide market economy. The interests of the worldwide market economy, quite contrary to all of the teachings of the colonists, are exactly the interests that promise to create a crisis for humanity in the decades to come.

The dialectical opposite of that process would be the rekindling, on a planetary basis, of locally based culture. Prior to the advent of colonialism, culture was defined as the way of life by which people survived within their own environment, and their own environment was defined as the area in which they lived. Thus the process of survival involved the use of locally

121

developed technologies that met the specific needs of the area. It was mentioned earlier that technologies have political cousins, and locally developed technologies have cousins, too. Decentralized technologies that meet the needs of the people those technologies serve will necessarily give life to a different kind of political structure, and it is safe to predict that the political structure that results will be anticolonial in nature.

Colonialism is at the heart of the impending world crisis. The development of liberation technologies, many of which already exist but have been largely ignored by the political movements (even the anticolonial political movements), are a necessary part of the decolonization process. Liberation technologies are those technologies that can be implemented by a specific people in a specific locality and free those people from dependency on multinational corporations and the governments that multinational corporations control. Liberation technologies are those that meet people's needs within the parameters defined by the cultures they themselves created (or create), and which have no dependency upon the world marketplace. Windmills can be a form of liberation technology, as can water wheels, solar collectors, biomass plants, woodlots, underground home construction—the list is very long.

Colonialism, as we know it, was the product of centuries of social, economic, and political development in the West. For hundreds of years, what have been euphemistically called "folk cultures" have been under pressure from a variety of sources, including warlords, kings, popes, and large landowners, who found it in their interest to exploit the labor and lands of the poor and the dispossessed. That process is still taking place today, although it has been refined to the point where the exploitation is in the hands of huge multinational corporations that continue to reap profits at the expense of the world's poor.

It is possible to make a strong argument that food shortages are almost entirely the product of colonial interests. Areas of land in the third world, usually the most productive farming areas, today produce exclusively export crops, while the Indigenous peoples, and even the descendants of the colonizers, go hungry, laboring in the coffee, banana, and other plantations of the multinationals. Political movements that have sought to correct those wrongs generally have attempted to overthrow the state, because they correctly saw the state as the tool of oppression and the repository of excess wealth for the interests of the exploiters.

Most of the past "liberation movements" have not been successful in correcting the most horrendous wrongs of colonialism, however, because they assumed that the problem lies solely in the fact that private interests controlled the state for their own benefit. The error of most such movements lies in the fact that they sought to liberate the country from living human beings, much as history assumes that Julius Caesar was somehow significant to the history of the West. They failed to understand that it did not matter whether Del Monte grew sugarcane or a liberated government grew sugarcane; the problem was that export crops do not meet the needs of Indigenous peoples. Most liberation efforts, therefore, recreate in some form the dependency that they sought to replace. They do not attempt to develop even the concept of liberation technologies, and they do not understand the need to become independent of the world market economy, because the world market economy is ultimately controlled by interests that seek power or profit and do not respond to the needs of the world's peoples.

Given the impending world crisis in the areas of food and energy, a comprehensive strategy for survival will include a concept of liberation technologies that free peoples from dependency on economies that are controlled by external interests. Liberation technologies have political cousins, just as colonizing technologies have, and those political cousins need careful consideration. Liberation technologies are accompanied by liberation political structures and liberation theologies. Of these two entities, colonized peoples in the West would be well advised to place considerable energy into the creation of true liberation theologies as a very high priority.

Liberation theologies are belief systems that challenge the assumption, widely held in the West, that the Earth is simply a commodity that can be exploited thoughtlessly by humans for the purpose of material acquisition within an ever-expanding economic framework. A liberation theology will develop in people a consciousness that all life on Earth is sacred and that the sacredness of life is the key to human freedom and survival. It will be obvious to many non-Western peoples that it is the renewable quality of Earth's ecosystems that makes life possible for human beings on this planet, and that if anything is sacred, if anything determines both the quality and future possibility of life for our species on this planet, it is that renewable quality of life.

The renewable quality—the sacredness of every living thing, that which connects human beings to the place they inhabit—that quality is the single most liberating aspect of our environment. Life is renewable and all the things that support life are renewable, and they are renewed by a force greater than any government's, greater than any living or historical thing. A consciousness of the web that holds all things together, the spiritual element that connects us to reality and the manifestation of

123

that power to renew that is present in the existence of an eagle or a mountain snow fall, that consciousness was the first thing that was destroyed by the colonizers.

A strategy for survival must include a liberation theology—call it a philosophy or cosmology if you will, but we believe it to be a theology—or humankind will simply continue to view the Earth as a commodity and will continue to seek more efficient ways to exploit that which they have not come to respect. If these processes continue unabated and unchanged at the foundation of the colonizer's ideology, our species will never be liberated from the undeniable reality that we live on a planet of limited resources, and sooner or later we will exploit our environment beyond its ability to renew itself.

Our strategy for survival is to create and implement liberation technologies that are consistent with and complementary to a liberation theology that arises out of our culture and is the product of the Natural World. It happens that we, the Haudenosaunee, have fallen heir to a liberation political structure that may be the oldest continuously operating governmental system in the world. We know that our traditional world view and our political structure were largely products of the technological and world view elements of our society.

The Haudenosaunee presented three papers to the Non-Governmental Organizations of the United Nations at Geneva, Switzerland, in 1977. Those papers were intended to introduce the people of the Western world to our understanding of the history of the West and the prospects for the future. We have taken many steps since the presentation of those papers to begin the process by which we may provide for the future of our people. Many of our communities are struggling against colonialism in all of its forms. We have established food co-ops, survival schools, alternative technology projects, adult education programs, agricultural projects, and crafts programs, and serious efforts at cultural revitalization are underway.

Sotsisowah

Afterword:
Indigenous into the 21st Century

A victory of substantial proportions was won on the final year of the twentieth century when the United Nations Economic and Social Council adopted a resolution establishing a Permanent Forum for Indigenous peoples within the international body. Although some still wonder about the worth of international representation, it is undeniable that the effort to reach out beyond the national borders that contain them has yielded some important results for tribal peoples.

In 1977, on the occasion of the first major meeting of Indigenous peoples at the United Nations in Geneva, Switzerland, as documented in this new edition of the much reprinted *A Basic Call to Consciousness*, few people in the world were interested in the rights of Native nations. Just five years earlier, a case in Colombia had given evidence of the level of infamy and disdain to which Indian people were being subjected. In that instance, a gang of cowboys had lured a small tribe of Indians out of the forest with the promise of a feast. As the Native guests ate, the cowboys fell upon them, killing sixteen, including women and children. This atrocious act came to the public's attention and the cowboys were charged with murder; however, they were later acquitted of their crime. "They did not know," the cowboy's lawyer argued successfully, "that it was wrong to kill Indians."

In Brazil, Bolivia, Paraguay, Guatemala, Mexico, and every other country in the Western Hemisphere with Indigenous populations, rapid depletion of forest was eradicating tribe after tribe from ancestral lands. When this type of rapacious development was opposed by tribes, severe repression often followed, including massacres of whole villages.

In the United States and Canada, the scale of anti-Indian carnage was not at massacre levels; nevertheless, a major current of intolerance and racism against Indians had generated high levels of violence. In several Western states with significant Indian populations, murder of Indians by whites met with lenience in the courts all too frequently. In a policy climate still bent on dispossession of lands and other tribal resources, the Native movement exploded into Alcatraz, the Trail of Broken Treaties Caravan, the challenge at Wounded Knee, and many other confrontational events and situations that signaled the need to seek strategic alliances and proper legal forums everywhere possible.

As coeditors of the national Indian newspaper, *Akwesasne Notes*, during those years, John Mohawk and I, along with Katsi Cook, Carol Cornelious, Daniel Thomas (Rokwaho), Mary Muñoz, with the help of many other contributors, shared the bimonthly task of assembling, editing, and writing the news and perspectives of the Native world, often while hosting delegations of chiefs, clanmothers, and Native activists and journalists from around the globe. I remember the chiefs from the various Haudenosaunee nations coming to ask John to write these pieces, and how they later showed up to have the articles read to them. They would ask about the history, because most of all they wanted to know—as old Joe Mitchell, Turtle Clan chief from Akwesasne, asked us one night—"What makes the white man act the way he does in the world? What in their history makes them at war with the Earth?" As it turned out, in Geneva the Indian elders from the Southern Hemisphere had (and continue to have) the same questions.

Those years were the heyday of a major movement that has been developing for two generations over the nearly thirty years since the 1977 conference. Oren Lyons has described the North American Indian "Unity Caravans" of the 1960s and 1970s. Simultaneously in Latin America, Indigenous "runners" from the southern countries had begun to come north. One runner is the Mapuche veteran Nilo Cayuqueo, who as a young man was sent out by his elders to carry their word to other Native people. (Cayuqueo, among others, carried their message to Geneva in 1977). As well, northern Native nations, prominently the Iroquois and delegations of Lakota, Pueblo, and Hopi, among others, were quietly traveling south during those years. Visionary leaders, like Reuben Snake of the Winnebago, traveled Mexico seeking contact with Native leaders there. Meetings of Maya and Mohawk elders occurred in 1975–76 that became a cornerstone of a people-to-people alliance that has lasted over a generation. In Canada, a current of outreach instigated by Chief George Manuel would become known as the "Fourth World" movement. This first early dialogue with Indigenous peoples immediately went beyond the international concept of the Third World, thus declaring the existence of a Fourth World of

Indigenous peoples. As John Mohawk writes, in 1975 the International Indian Treaty Council emerged out of meetings hosted by the American Indian Movement.

Delegations from North America were large at the 1977 meeting. Prominently, the Lakota Treaty Council and the Haudenosaunee chiefs and clanmothers were represented, and a medicine man from Oklahoma, Creek elder Phillip Deere, became a voice for millions when, holding high his medicine bundle, he declared in Geneva: "We, the Indigenous peoples, are the evidence of the Western Hemisphere. No matter how small a group they may be, each of them has the right to be who they are."

The expressions of culture-bearing elders like Phillip Deere, Leon Shenandoah, Art Solomon, and David Monongye, and the vision of Native thinkers and activists like Larry Red Shirt, Dan Bomberry, Lee Lyons, Ingrid Washinawatok, and the lawyer Howard Berman (to name just some of those who have passed on) in North America, combined with parallel representations of the delegates from Latin America (some of whom later fell to the wars of the 1980s), formed the basis of the language of Indigenous peoples' rights that has emerged in the international arena.

While it is true that no Native nation has yet to achieve status as a member nation of the United Nations, this remains a goal for many Indigenous peoples. It is not, however, the only important benefit of international recognition and networking. The language that develops in these dialogues around concepts of sovereignty, nation-to-nation protocols, and codes of interaction between governments and political representatives is also shared internationally by lawyers and bureaucrats; it makes its way to academic and higher educational programs; and it helps create a climate of deeper respect.

Most importantly, the "Draft Declaration on the Rights of Indigenous Peoples" has been under discussion in international circles since 1977. This very process of discussion of the Draft Declaration within the very slow, incremental approach toward adoption, which some critics use to disparage the international effort, is a victory in itself. It is precisely this ongoing and never-ending discussion that has educated thousands of international officials from dozens of countries about the existence, hopes, aspirations, and many contributions of Native peoples.

The movement sparked in 1977 has been useful in direct ways. Through the 1980s, as the wars in Central America evolved into slaughter campaigns against Indian communities, networking by Indigenous peoples often was fortified by the forums at the United Nations. During those years at the *Akwesasne Notes*, at the instruction of the traditional chiefs council of the Mohawk Nation, we monitored dozens of situations involving violations of human rights—many quite horrendous. We found that our tools of communication—whether newspapers, telephone trees, or the many traveling groups that emerged from our camps to visit universities and reservations throughout the United States, Canada, and even Central America—could be central to the survival of the tribal nations. More than a few lives were saved and several impending atrocities were circumvented due to the communications work of the Emergency Response International Network (ERIN) from 1979 to 1984. Sometimes the ideological and political debates within the Indian international movement, as was the case during the Miskito-Sandinista War—were as painful as they were deeply instructive.

As peace dawned on the traumatized region in the early 1990s, most of that same movement supported and applauded the awarding of the Nobel Peace Prize for 1992 to Rigoberta Menchu Tum, the Maya activist and author. The awarding of the Nobel Prize to an Indigenous woman symbolized an opening to crucial political space for Guatemala's Maya people; after horrible suffering, they would never again be invisible or voiceless.

By 1992, the Fourth World movement had expanded to represent the more than 300 million Indigenous peoples worldwide, including at least 40 million in the Americas. That same year, Indigenous peoples' cultural and practical knowledge of ecological factors in their traditional territories was recognized at the United Nations Conference on Environment and Development (UNCED). And three years later, when the United Nations opened its program of activities for the International Decade of Indigenous Peoples (1995-2004), a main objective of the Decade was the establishment of a Permanent Forum at the United Nations. The United States, once a stumbling block to international Indigenous rights, voted in full support of the forum.

In the South, several countries with major populations, including Mexico, Guatemala, Bolivia, Ecuador, and Peru, have seen Indian-led movements exercise significant influence on their national societies, from the Zapatista movement in Mexico, which challenged globalization with a bang, to the political upsurges in Bolivia and Ecuador that have collapsed and elected national presidents. In the North, a major economic explosion has occurred, with over two hundred tribal nations gaining rapidly on financial independence and growing power through sovereignty-protected, highly profitable gaming enterprises. Even some of the Indian leaders at Geneva in 1977, such as the New York Oneida Ray Halbritter and the Wisconsin Oneida Artley Skenandore, went on to run major tribal businesses. These two trends from the North and South are only now starting to merge as

In Geneva: (left to right) Art Montour, Mohawk; Chief Frank Abrams, Seneca; Chief Louie Thompson, Mohawk, Chief Leo Henry, Tuscarora; Chief Loran Thompson, Mohawk; Aaron Oakes, Mohawk; Chief Corbett Sundown, Seneca; Chief Stuart Patterson, Tuscarora; Audrey Shenandoah, Deer Clan Mother, Onondaga; Chief Jimmy Leaf, Cayuga; Ray Halbritter, Oneida; and Chief Oren Lyons, Faithkeeper, Onondaga.

tribes from both hemispheres continue to engage in dialogues during the international meetings every May in New York City.

Proposed in 1993 at the Vienna World Conference on Human Rights and approved in 2004, the Permanent Forum now provides Indigenous peoples of the world (delegates from over seventy countries attend) with the opportunity to inject the unique voice of the Native peoples of the world into the global human discourse.

In the Americas, certainly, borders separating Indian peoples—as psychological, as linguistic, and as legalistic as those of national frontiers—are coming down. A sense of "all our relations" is increasingly apparent in the communications between Indians throughout North America, Central America, the Caribbean, and South America. It is a refreshing trend.

I am happy to note the recent (2003) repatriation of Taíno human remains from the United States' Smithsonian Institution's National Museum of the American Indian to a small Indian enclave in Cuba's eastern mountains, the community of Caridad de los Indios. Navajo,

Mohawk, Algonquin, Kaw, Paiute, Chicano, and other peoples, including scholars and participants from several countries, witnessed the unique ceremony, which coalesced the forces of many people to guarantee its success.

The reinterment gave evidence, too, of the survival of Native traditional cultures and peoples in the most remote and unpredictable places in the Americas. For the small enclave of Taíno descendents at Caridad de los Indios, high up in the mountains of Guantanamo, Cuba, to finally make themselves known and respected at an international level, after nearly five hundred years of supposed extinction, is a marvel in itself. That a repatriation of our ancestral remains could be conducted between two countries still in the throes of ideological hostility gives evidence of the growing level of direct cooperation going on among Indian peoples of the countries of Latin America and North America.

Unlike the situation at the start of the twentieth century, when many considered Indians "the Vanishing Americans," there is nothing crestfallen about the present moment for the peoples of Indian Country and the Native Americas. The Indian peoples of the Americas are relatives to each other and constitute the primary cultural and sometimes human foundation of the modern American republics. All of this is quite different now as a result of the intense Indigenous effort for self-determination over the past thirty years. These are trends that usher in a new era of possibility for Native nations.

José Barreiro
Crows Hill, New York

Acknowledgements

Special thanks goes out to the numerous people who worked hard to bring this revised edition of *Basic Call to Consciousness* to fruition. Thank you to Tonya Gonnella Frichner (Onondaga Nation–Snipe Clan) president and founder of the American Indian Law Alliance, and the hard working folks at the American Indian Law Alliance (www.ailanyc.org). The American Indian Law Alliance organizes and advocates on a national and international level on behalf of and with Indigenous peoples from around the world. Thank you to Chief Oren Lyons (Onondaga–Wolf Clan), John Mohawk (Seneca), and José Barreiro (Taíno Nation of the Antilles) for their new contributions. Thank you to Stefan Disko who provided valuable fact-checking, as well as careful research for the endnotes and bibliography. Jerry Hutchens coordinated efforts. Thank you to the dozens of folks who donated time and talent. This work has been a labor of love. May it bring understanding and change.

Notes

The Haudenosaunee: A Nation Since Time Immemorial

1. *Treaty of Fort Stanwix*, October 22, 1784, U.S.-Six Nations, 7 Stat. 15. For more on the Treaty of Fort Stanwix, see G. Peter Jemison and Anna M. Schein, eds., *Treaty of Canandaigua 1794: 200 Years of Treaty Relations between the Iroquois Confederacy and the United States* (Santa Fe: Clear Light Publishers, 2000); and Barbara Graymont, *The Iroquois in the American Revolution* (Syracuse: Syracuse University Press, 1972).

2. On the New York State treaties of this period, see Laurence M. Hauptman, *Conspiracy of Interests: Iroquois Dispossession and the Rise of New York State* (Syracuse: Syracuse University Press, 1999); and Barbara Graymont, *The Iroquois in the American Revolution*.

3. See Jemison/Schein, *Treaty of Canandaigua 1794;* and Hauptman, *Conspiracy of Interests*.

4. The St. Regis Tribal Council, an "elected" entity that claims jurisdictional authority on the "U.S." side of Akwesasne. Although members of the community at Akwesasne have consistently resisted this form of government, the St. Regis Tribal Council received federal recognition in 1972 and has become the government recognized by New York State and the U.S. federal government as the legal entity at Akwesasne. The traditional people of the Mohawk Nation continue to be represented by the Mohawk Nation Council of Chiefs, which is the connection of the Mohawk people to the Grand Council of the Haudenosaunee.

5. In 1899, the government of Canada created the St. Regis Band Council (now called Mohawk Council of Akwesasne), and imposed it on the Mohawks by force of arms. The Mohawk Council of Akwesasne is an "elected" body that claims jurisdictional authority on the "Canadian" district of Akwesasne. See Doug George-Kanentiio, *Iroquois Culture & Commentary* (Santa Fe: Clear Light Publishers, 2000), 127-128, 179-180.

6. *Citizenship Act of 1924*, 43 Stat. 253, 8 U.S.C. 1401(a)(2). Note, however, that by virtue of various federal statutes and treaties, a significant number of Native

people had already received United States citizenship before 1924 (with or without their consent). See *General Allotment Act*, Sec. 6, 24 Stat. 388 (1887), 25 U.S.C. 331 et seq. (Indians "to whom allotments shall have been made"); *Act of August 9, 1888*, ch. 818, sec. 2, 25 Stat. 392, 25 U.S.C. 182 ("marriage between white men and Indian women"); and *Treaty with the Potawatomi, November 15, 1861*, 12 Stat. 1191, Art. 3 ("competent" male heads of families). For more on these issues, see Laurence M. Hauptman, "Congress, Plenary Power, and the American Indian, 1870 to 1992," in Jemison/Schein, *Treaty of Canandaigua*, 321-326; and Vine Deloria, Jr. and Clifford M. Lytle, *American Indians, American Justice* (Austin: University of Texas Press, 1988), 217-222.

7. In 1920, the Canadian *Indian Act* had been amended to allow the compulsory enfranchisement of (i.e. imposition of citizenship on) "any Indian, male or female, over the age of twenty-one years . . . fit for enfranchisement." According to the amendment, enfranchised Indians were no longer to be "deemed . . . Indians within the meaning of any laws relating to Indians," and were to "have, possess and enjoy all the legal powers, rights and privileges of His Majesty's other subjects" (*An Act to amend the Indian Act, 10-11 Geo V, 1920 c.50*, assented to July 1, 1920). The amendment was repealed two years later but was reintroduced in slightly modified form in 1933, and retained until the major revision of the Indian Act in 1951. A further modification was made in 1951 (and retained until 1985) that allowed the compulsory enfranchisement of Indian women who married non-Aboriginal, Métis, Inuit, or unregistered Indian men. See Royal Commission on Aboriginal Peoples, *Report of the Royal Commission on Aboriginal Peoples* (Ottawa: Canada Communication Group, 1996), Vol. 1(2), chapter 9, para. 9.3. See also Clinton Rickard (editor: Barbara Graymont), *Fighting Tuscarora: The Autobiography of Chief Clinton Rickard*, (Syracuse: Syracuse University Press, 1973), 59.

8. For more detailed accounts, see Grace Li Xiu Woo, "Canada's Forgotten Founders: The Modern Significance of the Haudenosaunee (Iroquois) Application for Membership in the League of Nations," in *Law, Social Justice & Global Development Journal (LGD) 2003 (1)* (Coventry: University of Warwick, 2003), http://elj.warwick.ac.uk/global/issue/2003-1/woo.htm, 9-10; Laurence M. Hauptman, *The Iroquois and the New Deal* (Syracuse: Syracuse University Press, 1981), 15; and Rickard, *Autobiography*, 60-62.

9. 48 Stat. 984, 25 U.S.C. 461-479. See Deloria/Lytle, *American Indians, American Justice*, 12-15; Vine Deloria, Jr., *Behind the Trail of Broken Treaties: An Indian Declaration of Independence* (New York: Dell Publishing, 1974), 187-206; and Hauptman, "Congress, Plenary Power, and the American Indian," 326-329. For a discussion of the IRA in the context of the Haudenosaunee, see Hauptman, *The Iroquois and the New Deal.*

10. *Act of July 2, 1948* (62 Stat. 1224; 25 U.S.C. 232) (criminal jurisdiction); *Act of September 13, 1950* (64 Stat. 845; 25 U.S.C. 233) (civil jurisdiction). These two acts predate the more general application of state jurisdiction to Native peoples embodied in Public Law 280 of August 15, 1953, which was largely based on the acts of 1948 and 1950. Public Law 280 was one of the cornerstones of the

Termination Policy of the 1950s. See also Laurence M. Hauptman, *The Iroquois Struggle for Survival: World War II to Red Power* (Syracuse: Syracuse University Press, 1986), 45-64; and Chief Irving Powless Jr., "The Haudenosaunee, Yesterday and Today: A Conflict of Concepts and Laws," in *Buffalo Law Review* 46, No. 3 (1998), 1083-1084.

11. For more detailed accounts, see Hauptman, *The Iroquois Struggle for Survival*; John Mohawk, "Epilogue," in Paul Wallace, *White Roots of Peace: The Iroquois Book of Life* (Santa Fe: Clear Light Publishers, 1994), 139-150; and Rickard, *Autobiography*, 138-152.

12. See Powless, "The Haudenosaunee, Yesterday and Today," 1086-1087.

13. See Notes, A Basic Call to Consciousness: The Haudenosaunee Address to the Western World, Policies of Oppression in the Name of Democracy, note 16 and accompanying text.

14. The conference was held at UN facilities, but was not officially a UN conference. For reports and documents related to this conference, see *Akwesasne Notes*, Vol. 9, No. 5 (December 1977); International Indian Treaty Council, "The Geneva Conference–Official Report by: International Indian Treaty Council" (Special Issue: *Treaty Council News*, October 1977, Vol. 1, No. 7); and Institute for the Development of Indian Law, "International NGO Conference on Discrimination Against Indigenous Peoples in the Americas–1977," in *American Indian Journal* 3 (1977). For retrospectives on the significance and impact of this Conference, see Ingrid Washinawatok, "International Emergence: Twenty-One Years at the United Nations," in *New York City Law Review* 3 (1999), 41-57; and Sharon H. Venne, *Our Elders Understand Our Rights: Evolving International Law Regarding Indigenous Rights* (Penticton: Theytus Books, Ltd., 1998), 107-163. On the recent establishment of a Permanent Forum for Indigenous peoples within the United Nations, see IWGIA (International Work Group for Indigenous Affairs), "The Permanent Forum on Indigenous Issues," in IWGIA, *The Indigenous World 2001-2002* (Copenhagen: IWGIA, 2002), 444-451.

Deskaheh: An Iroquois Patriot's Fight for International Recognition

1. This is a revised version of an essay that originally appeared under the title "I Am a Cayuga" in Carl Carmer, *Dark Trees to the Wind: A Cycle of York State Years* (New York: William Sloan Associates, 1949), 105-117. It was also included in the pamphlet *Deskaheh: Iroquois Statesman and Patriot*, first published in the 1950s by Akwesasne Mohawk Counselor Organization, and later reprinted by *Akwesasne Notes* in 1976.

2. *Haldimand Treaty/Deed*, October 25, 1784. See Graymont, *The Iroquois in the American Revolution*, 293-294, 299. The rights to the lands granted by the Haldimand Treaty were further guaranteed by the *Simcoe Treaty/Deed* ("Patent"

issued by Lieutenant-Governor J. Graves Simcoe on January 14, 1793). See Beverley K. Jacobs (Assembly of First Nations–British Columbia), "The Effect of Delgamuukw on Treaties in Ontario" (January 2001), research paper posted on the Delgamuukw/Gisday'wa National Process Web site, http://www. delgamuukw.org /research/ontariotreaties.pdf.

3. *Treaty of Amity, Commerce and Navigation* (between Britain and the United States), concluded on November 19, 1794, ratified on June 24, 1795, proclaimed on February 29, 1796. Article III of the Treaty provides in part: "It is agreed that it shall at all times be free to His Majesty's subjects, and to the citizens of the United States, and also to the Indians dwelling on either side of the said boundary line, freely to pass and repass by land or inland navigation, into the respective territories and countries of the two parties, on the continent of America . . . and to navigate all the lakes, rivers and waters thereof, and freely to carry on trade and commerce with each other . . . No duty of entry shall ever be levied by either party on peltries brought by land or inland navigation into the said territories respectively, nor shall the Indians passing or repassing with their own proper goods and effects of whatever nature, pay for the same any impost or duty whatever." See also Rickard, *Autobiography*, 69-89.

4. During World War I (1914-1918), many Aboriginal people in Canada voluntarily enlisted in the Canadian army even before official permission for Indians to enlist was given in December 1915. At this point, formal recruiting campaigns for Aboriginal volunteers got under way, including at residential schools. This led to considerable suspicion and opposition among Aboriginal people. Then in 1917, as general enlistment slowed and manpower needs increased, the Canadian government passed the *Military Service Act* of August 29, 1917, which provided for registration and conscription of all male British subjects from twenty to forty-five years of age, including Aboriginal people. No consideration was given to status Indians' lack of citizenship or to treaty membership. The possibility of conscription was protested by Aboriginal communities and leaders, and on January 17, 1918, a provision was passed that exempted Aboriginal men from combative service (P.C. 111), on the basis that they were not qualified to vote. See Royal Commission on Aboriginal Peoples, *Report of the Royal Commission*, Vol. 1(2), chapter 12, para. 2; and R. Scott Sheffield, *A Search for Equity: A Study of the Treatment Accorded to First Nations Veterans and Dependents of the Second World War and the Korean Conflict* (Report prepared for the National Roundtable on First Nations Veterans' Issues, April 2001), 5.

5. See Rickard, *Autobiography*, 61; and Woo, "Canada's Forgotten Founders," 7.

6. The *Haldimand Treaty/Deed*, October 25, 1784.

7. For a detailed account of these incidents, see Woo, "Canada's Forgotten Founders," 7-8; and Rickard, *Autobiography*, 60.

8. See Woo, "Canada's Forgotten Founders," 8-9. See also Washinawatok, "International Emergence," 42-43; Rickard, *Autobiography*, 61-62; and Hauptman, *The Iroquois and the New Deal*, 16.

9. See *The Redman's Appeal For Justice*, August 6, 1923, document submitted by Deskaheh to the League of Nations (League of Nations file 33687/28075); and *Chief Deskaheh Tells Why He Is Over Here Again*, London, August 1923. Both documents are contained in the George P. Decker Collection, The Lavery Library, St. John Fisher College, Rochester, New York, as well as the Howard R. Berman Collection, Charles B. Sears Law Library, University of Buffalo, New York.

10. See Rickard, *Autobiography*, 61-62; Hauptman, *The Iroquois and the New Deal*, 15; and Woo, "Canada's Forgotten Founders," 9.

11. *Haldimand Treaty/Deed*, October 25, 1784. See Notes, Deskaheh: An Iroquois Patriot's Fight for International Recognition, note 2.

12. See Rickard, *Autobiography*, 63-66.

13. Deskaheh, radio broadcast over station WHAM (Rochester, NY), March 10, 1925.

A Basic Call to Consciousness: The Haudenosaunee Address to the Western World

Spiritualism, the Highest Form of Political Consciousness

1. Paulo Freire, *Pedagogy of the Oppressed* (New York: Continuum, 1970).

The Obvious Fact of Our Continuing Existence

1. On the influences of the Great Law of Peace on the U.S. Constitution, see Chief Oren Lyons and John Mohawk, eds., *Exiled in the Land of the Free: Democracy, Indian Nations, and the U.S. Constitution* (Santa Fe: Clear Light Publishers, 1992); Bruce E. Johansen, *Forgotten Founders: How the American Indian Helped Shape Democracy* (Harvard and Boston: The Harvard Common Press, 1982); Bruce E. Johansen, *Debating Democracy: Native American Legacy of Freedom* (Santa Fe: Clear Light Publishers, 1998); José Barreiro, ed., *Indian Roots of American Democracy* (Ithaka: Akwe:kon Press, Cornell University, 1992); and Greg Schaaf, *The Great Law of Peace and the Constitution of the United States of America* (Pamphlet published by Tree of Peace Society, 1987). See also *Senate Concurrent Resolution 76* of September 16, 1987, which recognizes and acknowledges the contribution of the Iroquois Confederacy of Nations to the development of the U.S. Constitution; and United States Congress Senate Select Committee on Indian Affairs Report 100-565, *Acknowledging the contribution of the Iroquois Confederacy of Nations to the Development of the United States Constitution . . .* (Washington, DC: U.S. Government Printing Office, 1988).

2. See Lewis Henry Morgan, *Ancient Society, or Researches in the Lines of Human Progress from Savagery, through Barbarism to Civilization* (London: Macmillan & Co., 1877);

and Lewis H. Morgan, *League of the Ho-de'-no-sau-nee, or Iroquois* (Rochester: Sage & Brother, 1851).

3. See Karl Marx and Lawrence Krader, eds., *The Ethnological Notebooks of Karl Marx: Studies of Morgan, Phear, Maine, Lubbock* (Assen: Van Gorcum, 1972); and Johansen, *Forgotten Founders*, 19, 121-123. See also Frederick Engels, *The Origin of the Family, Private Property and the State: In Light of the Researches of Lewis H. Morgan* (New York: International Publishers, 1972; originally published 1884 in Hottingen-Zurich).

4. Eric R. Wolf, *Peasants* (Eaglewood Cliffs: Prentice-Hall, Foundations of Modern Anthropology Series, 1966), 11. See Cyril S. Belshaw, *Traditional Exchange and Modern Markets* (Eaglewood Cliffs: Prentice-Hall, Modernization of Traditional Societies Series, 1965), 53-54.

5. Alfred L. Kroeber, *Anthropology: Race, Language, Culture, Psychology, Prehistory— Revised Edition* (New York: Harcourt, Brace and Company, 1948), 284. See Margaret Park Redfield, ed., *Human Nature and the Study of Society: The Papers of Robert Redfield, Vol. 1* (Chicago: University of Chicago Press, 1962), I, 287.

6. Robert Redfield, *Peasant Society and Culture: An Anthropological Approach to Civilization* (Chicago: University of Chicago Press, 1956), 45-46.

7. Francis Jennings, *The Invasion of America: Indians, Colonialism, and the Cant of Conquest* (New York: W.W. Norton & Company, 1976), 105-106.

8. Jennings, *The Invasion of America*, 127.

9. Ibid.

10. In 1924, the government of Canada forcefully imposed the elective Band Council structure under the Indian Act on the "Six Nations Indian Band" of the Grand River Territory by Order in Council P.C. 1629, dated September 17, 1924. See Woo, "Canada's Forgotten Founders," 9-10; and Rickard, *Autobiography*, 60-62.

11. 48 Stat. 984, 25 U.S.C. 461-479. See Notes, The Haudenosaunee: A Nation Since Time Immemorial, note 9 and accompanying text.

12. Made in 1613. The Two Row Treaty was recorded by the Haudenosaunee in the Two Row Wampum Belt (Guswenta). Guswenta is a long belt of white and purple wampum beads: two long and parallel lines of purple, separated by three rows of white. The two purple lines in the belt symbolize the distinct identity of the two peoples and a mutual promise to coexist in peace without interference in the internal affairs of the other. On the symbolism of the Guswenta, see Chief Irving Powless Jr., "Treaty Making," in Jemison/Schein, *Treaty of Canandaigua*, 22-23; Oren R. Lyons, "The American Indian in the Past," in Lyons/Mohawk, *Exiled in the Land of the Free*, 40-42; and Robert W. Venables, "Some Observations on the Treaty of Canandaigua," in Jemison/Schein, *Treaty of Canandaigua*, 107-108.

13. U.S. Const., Art. I, Sec. 8, cl. 3.

14. See Deloria/Lytle, *American Indians, American Justice*, 40-45; Deloria, *Behind the Trail of Broken Treaties*, 141-160; and Indian Law Resource Center, "United States

Denial of Indian Property Rights: A Study in Lawless Power and Racial Discrimination," in National Lawyers Guild Committee on Native American Struggles, ed., *Rethinking Indian Law* (New Haven: The Advocate Press, 1982), 24.

15. See Robert T. Coulter, "The Denial of Legal Remedies to Indian Nations Under U.S. Law," in National Lawyers Guild Committee on Native American Struggles, *Rethinking Indian Law*, 103-107.

16. See Felix S. Cohen, *Handbook of Federal Indian Law* (Washington, DC: U.S. Government Printing Office, 1942), 421 (chapter 22, section 1, F.5./6.); Laurence M. Hauptman, "The State's Men, the Salvation Seekers, and the Seneca: The Supplemental Treaty of Buffalo Creek, 1842," in *New York History* 78, No.1 (January 1997): 80-81.

17. In the case of the Cayuga Nation, in particular three "treaties" with the state of New York in 1789 (*Treaty of Albany, February 25, 1789*), in 1795 (*Treaty of Cayuga Ferry, July 27, 1795*), and in 1807 (*Treaty of Albany, May 30, 1807*). In the case of the Oneida Nation, the "treaties" with the state of New York in 1785 (*Treaty of Fort Herkimer, June 28, 1785*) and 1788 (*Treaty of Fort Schuyler, September 22, 1788*); and a long series of about twenty-five other written "agreements" with the state of New York between 1795 and 1846. See generally, Hauptman, *Conspiracy of Interests;* and Graymont, *The Iroquois in the American Revolution.* For details about the Cayuga treaties, see Clint Halftown, "The Haudenosaunee Cayuga Nation Land Claim: Cayuga Nation v. New York," in *Buffalo Law Review* 46, No. 3 (1998), 1091-1095; and New York State Assembly, *Report of the Special Committee to Investigate the Indian Problem of the State of New York*—Appointed by the Assembly of 1888 (Albany: Troy Press, 1889) ["Whipple Report"], 216-229. For details about the Oneida treaties, see Jack Campisi, "The Treaty Period, 1783-1838," in Jack Campisi and Laurence M. Hauptman, eds., *The Oneida Indian Experience* (Syracuse: Syracuse University Press, 1988), 48-64; Laurence M. Hauptman and L. Gordon McLester III, eds., *The Oneida Indian Journey: From New York to Wisconsin, 1784-1860* (Madison: University of Wisconsin Press, 1999), 38-52, 85-89, 151-170; George C. Shattuck, *The Oneida Land Claims: A Legal History* (Syracuse: Syracuse University Press, 1991); and "Whipple Report," 234-265.

18. Conducted in Albany, New York, on March 29, 1797. In the United States referred to as "Treaty with the Mohawk" (7 Stat. 61).

19. See Cohen, *Handbook of Federal Indian Law*, 420-21 (chapter 22, section 1.F.); and Hauptman, *Conspiracy of Interests.* Also see Notes, A Basic Call to Consciousness: The Haudenosaunee Address to the Western World, Policies of Oppression in the Name of Democracy, note 6.

20. *General Allotment Act*, 24 Stat. 388 (1887), 25 U.S.C. 331 et seq. See Delos Sacket Otis, *The Dawes Act and the Allotment of Indian Lands* (Norman: University of Oklahoma Press, 1973); and Deloria/Lytle, *American Indians, American Justice*, 8-12. For the impact of the Dawes Act on the Iroquois, see Hauptman, *The Iroquois and the New Deal*, 5, 22, 71-72, 91-92.

21. *Citizenship Act of 1924*, 43 Stat. 253, 8 U.S.C. 1401(a)(2). See Notes, The Haudenosaunee: A Nation Since Time Immemorial, note 9 and accompanying text.

22. See Notes, Deskaheh: An Iroquois Patriot's Fight for International Recognition, note 10.

23. See Eileen Antone, "The Oneida Move to Canada," in Hauptman/McLester, *The Oneida Indian Journey*, 136.

24. See Notes, The Haudenosaunee: A Nation Since Time Immemorial, note 10.

25. Public Law 88-533 (August 31, 1964), 78 Stat. 738. For further details on the struggle around Kinzua Dam, see Joy A. Bilharz, *The Allegany Senecas and Kinzua Dam: Forced Relocation through Two Generations* (Lincoln: University of Nebraska Press, 1998); Hauptman, *The Iroquois Struggle for Survival*, 85-104; Hauptman, "Congress, Plenary Power, and the American Indian," 332-334; and Mohawk, "Epilogue," in Wallace, *White Roots of Peace*, 140-146.

26. Geneva.

27. See Rickard, *Autobiography*, 131-132: "Beginning in 1948 and for several years thereafter, representatives of the Six Nations Confederacy made an annual trip to the United Nations headquarters in New York City. We brought our message of peace to this world body and reminded the delegates we met that we were the first United Nations. In 1949, a group of us from the Six Nations attended the cornerstone laying of the UN building in Manhattan. In 1950, we presented a petition to the United Nations protesting the attempts of Canada, the United States, and the state of New York to assume jurisdiction over our Six Nations Confederacy and called attention to our opposition to the attempts of these foreign powers to assimilate our people. In 1952, we petitioned the United Nations to admit the Six Nations Confederacy to membership. This petition was pigeonholed."

28. The United Nations Conference on the Human Environment, Stockholm, June 5-12, 1972, the first major modern international gathering on human activities in relationship to the environment. The conference produced a set of principles in the Stockholm Declaration and led to the founding of the United Nations Environment Programme (UNEP). Among the Indigenous delegates attending this conference were Alice Papineau (Onondaga), Thomas Banyacya (Hopi), Tom Cook (Mohawk), and George Manuel (Shushwap).

Policies of Oppression in the Name of "Democracy"

1. *Treaty of Fort Stanwix*, October 22, 1784. See Notes, The Haudenosaunee: A Nation Since Time Immemorial, note 1.

2. See John C. Mohawk, "The Canandaigua Treaty in Historical Perspective," in Jemison/Schein, *Treaty of Canandaigua*, 48; and Graymont, *The Iroquois in the American Revolution*, 284.

3. See Graymont, *The Iroquois in the American Revolution*, 284; Anthony F.C. Wallace, *The Death and Rebirth of the Seneca* (New York: Alfred A. Knopf, 1970), 152; and Mohawk, "The Canandaigua Treaty in Historical Perspective," 48.

4. See Cohen, *Handbook of Federal Indian Law*, 420 (chapter 22, section 1, F.3.); and Reginald Horsman, "The Origins of Oneida Removal to Wisconsin, 1815-1822," in Hauptman/McLester, *The Oneida Indian Journey*, 53- 69.

5. *Treaty of Buffalo Creek* of January 15, 1838 (between the United States and "the New York Indians"), 7 Stat. 550. It is well established that the treaty was produced through bribery, coercion, and forgery, and it is generally considered as fraudulent. See Morgan, *League of the Ho-de'-no-sau-nee*, 32-34; Cohen, *Handbook of Federal Indian Law*, 420 (chapter 22, section 1, F.3.); Henry S. Manley, "Buying Buffalo from the Indians," in *New York History* 27 (July 1947), 313-329; Laurence M. Hauptman, "Four Eastern New Yorkers and Seneca Lands: A Study in Treaty-Making," in *Hudson Valley Regional Review* 13 (March 1996), 1-19; and Laurence Hauptman, *Tribes and Tribulations: Misconceptions about American Indians and Their Histories* (Albuquerque: University of New Mexico Press, 1995), chapter 4.

6. Under the terms of the 1838 treaty, the Senecas ceded all of their remaining homelands in New York (the reservations at Allegany, Cattaraugus, Tonawanda, and Buffalo Creek), and relinquished their rights to Menominee lands in Wisconsin that had been purchased for them by the U.S. government. In exchange, the United States granted the Iroquois (as a whole) and the Stockbridge-Munsee rights to a 1,824,000-acre reservation in Kansas. In addition, the Indians were to receive some money from the U.S. government. However, the Senecas denounced the treaty due to its fraudulent nature and refused to move to Kansas or leave their homelands in New York. In 1842, a supplemental "compromise" treaty, the *Treaty of Buffalo Creek of May 20, 1842* (7 Stat. 586), was concluded between the United States and the Senecas (without the consent of the Tonawanda chiefs). The Senecas regained the Allegany and Cattaraugus Reservations, but not the Buffalo Creek or Tonawanda Reservations. The Senecas on the Buffalo Creek Reservation, which was permanently lost, gradually moved to the other Seneca reservations. The Tonawanda Senecas, who did not recognize the treaties of either 1838 or 1842, still refused to move and on November 5, 1857, made another treaty with the United States (11 Stat. 735, 12 Stat. 991) that "allowed" them to repurchase part of their Reservation. See Cohen, *Handbook of Federal Indian Law*, 420 (chapter 22, section 1, F.3.); Hauptman, "The State's Men, the Salvation Seekers, and the Seneca: The Supplemental Treaty of Buffalo Creek, 1842," 51-82.

7. See infra note 15 and accompanying text.

8. See John Ehle, *Trail of Tears: The Rise and Fall of the Cherokee Nation* (New York: Doubleday, 1988); and Theda Purdue and Michael D. Green, *The Cherokee Removal: A Brief History with Documents* (New York: Bedford Books of St. Martin's Press, 1995).

9. *Act of March 3, 1871*, 16 Stat. 566, 25 U.S.C. 71. The whole clause reads as

follows: "*Provided,* That hereafter no Indian nation or tribe, within the territory of the United States shall be acknowledged or recognized as an independent nation, tribe, or power, with whom the United States may contract by treaty: *Provided further,* That nothing herein contained shall be construed to invalidate or impair the obligation of any treaty heretofore lawfully made and ratified with any such Indian nation or tribe . . . " This provision is still in effect.

10. *General Allotment Act,* 24 Stat. 388 (1887), 25 U.S.C. 331 et seq. See Notes, A Basic Call to Consciousness: The Haudenosaunee Address to the Western World, The Obvious Fact of Our Continued Existence, note 20.

11. As a result of the *Dawes Act* and subsequent legislation, American Indian land-holdings were reduced from 138 million to 52 million acres between 1887 and 1934. See Hauptman, "Congress, Plenary Power, and the American Indian," 321-327; Otis, *The Dawes Act and the Allotment of Indian Lands*; and Deloria/Lytle, *American Indians, American Justice,* 8-12.

12. See Jorge Noriega, "American Indian Education in the United States: Indoctrination for Subordination to Colonialism," in M. Annette Jaimes, ed., *The State of Native America: Genocide, Colonization, and Resistance* (Boston: South End Press, 1992), 371-402.

13. New York State Assembly, *Report of the Special Committee to Investigate the Indian Problem of the State of New York*—Appointed by the Assembly of 1888 (Albany: Troy Press, 1889). The "Whipple Report" concluded (at page 79): "These Indian people have been kept as 'wards' or children long enough. They should now be educated to be men, not Indians, and it is the earnest belief of the committee that when . . . the Indians of the State are absorbed into the great mass of the American people, then, and not before, will the 'Indian problem' be solved." On the Whipple Committee and its report, see Laurence M. Hauptman, "Seneca Nation of Indians v. Christy: A Background Study," in *Buffalo Law Review,* Vol. 46, No. 3 (Fall 1998), 948-953; and Hauptman, *The Iroquois in the Civil War,* 149-150.

14. *Citizenship Act of 1924,* 43 Stat. 253, 8 U.S.C. 1401(a)(2). See Notes, The Haudenosaunee: A Nation Since Time Immemorial, note 6 and accompanying text.

15. A series of Congressional Acts between 1953 and 1958, by which federal recognition of a total of 109 Native nations, or parts of nations, was unilaterally withdrawn. Services to these nations provided by the Bureau of Indian Affairs were transferred to other federal, state, or local governmental agencies, or to the Indian nations themselves. Civil and criminal jurisdiction, to varying degrees, were transferred to the respective states. The two cornerstones of the Termination Policy were *House Concurrent Resolution 108* of August 1, 1953 (67 Stat. B132) and *Public Law 280* of August 15, 1953 (67 Stat. 588-590). The underlying goals of the policy were to integrate Indians, *as individuals,* into the mainstream of American society; to extinguish the collective political existence of the Indian nations; to abolish treaty rights; and to end the federal government's responsibility for Indian affairs. See Hauptman, "Congress, Plenary Power, and the American Indian," 329-334; Deloria/Lytle, *American Indians,*

American Justice, 15-21; and Rebecca L. Robbins, "Self-Determination and Subordination: The Past, Present, and Future of American Indian Governance," in Jaimes, *The State of Native America*, 98-100. For a discussion of the Termination Policy in the context of the Haudenosaunee, see Hauptman, *The Iroquois Struggle for Survival*, 42-83.

16. The settlement of Ganienkeh was originally established in May 1974 by a number of Mohawks who occupied an abandoned girls' camp at Moss Lake in the Adirondacks in New York. In 1977, the people of Ganienkeh reached an agreement with the state of New York to resettle their community to a new site on Miner Lake near Altona, New York where it is still located today. See Greg Horn, "Ganienkeh celebrates 25th anniversary," in *The Eastern Door*, Vol. 8, No. 15 (May 7, 1999); Greg Horn, "Ganienkeh since 1977," in *The Eastern Door*, Vol. 8, No. 16 (May 14, 1999); Bruce E. Johansen and Barbara A. Mann, eds., *Encyclopedia of the Haudenosaunee (Iroquois Confederacy)* (Westport: Greenwood Press, 2000), 104; and Gail Landsman, *Sovereignty and Symbol: Indian-White Conflict at Ganienkeh* (Albuquerque: University of New Mexico Press, 1988).

17. In 1970, the Oneidas filed a lawsuit in federal court challenging the validity of a 1795 "treaty" between the state of New York and the Oneida Indian Nation, based on the 1790 *Trade and Intercourse Act* (1 Stat. 137, 25 U.S.C. 177) and federal common law principles regarding the protection of Indian lands, which exclude states from making treaties with Indians. In 1974, the U.S. Supreme Court ruled in a landmark decision that "Indian title is a matter of federal law and can be extinguished only with federal consent," and that the Oneidas could maintain a course of action in federal court pursuant to the *Trade and Intercourse Act* (see *Oneida Indian Nation v. County of Oneida*, 414 U.S. 661). The case then proceeded to trial on the merits, and in 1985 the U.S. Supreme Court held in *County of Oneida v. Oneida Indian Nation of New York* (470 U.S. 226) that the Oneidas' land had been taken illegally in the 1795 "treaty." Since then, the parties have attempted to negotiate a settlement, but so far there has not been a final resolution. For the history of the Oneida land claims, see Hauptman, *The Iroquois Struggle for Survival*, 179-203; Arlinda Locklear, "The Oneida Land Claims: A Legal Overview," in Christopher Vecsey and William A. Starna, eds., *Iroquois Land Claims* (Syracuse: Syracuse University Press, 1988); Shattuck, *The Oneida Land Claims*; Arlinda Locklear, "The Buffalo Creek Treaty of 1838 and Its Legal Implications for Oneida Indian Land Claims," in Hauptman/McLester, *The Oneida Indian Journey*, 85-89; and Curtis Berkey, "The Legal Basis for Iroquois Land Claims," in *Akwe:kon Journal* 10, No. 1 (Spring 1993), 23-25; and John Tahsuda, "The Oneida Land Claim: Yesterday and Today," in *Buffalo Law Review* 46, No. 3 (1998), 1001-1009.

18. After the U.S. Supreme Court's 1974 decision in the Oneida case (see supra note 17), the Cayuga Nation negotiated with New York State regarding two "treaties" in 1795 and 1807, in which the Cayugas ceded 64,027 acres, constituting all of their remaining homelands, to New York. Both of these "treaties" were entered into by New York State in patent violation of the 1790 *Trade and Intercourse Act*, which forbade states to make treaties with Indians. In 1979, New York State and the Cayuga Nation entered into a formal settlement agreement.

However, the settlement was not approved by Congress, and in 1980 the Cayuga Nation filed a federal lawsuit against 11,000 New York State defendants for 64,027 acres of land and $350 million in damages (*Cayuga Indian Nation of New York v. Cuomo*). In 1992 the federal government joined the suit as a plaintiff-intervenor on behalf of the Cayuga Nation, which enabled the Cayugas to sue the state of New York. U.S. District Judge Neal McCurn ruled that the Cayugas had a valid claim to the land because it was acquired by the state in violation of federal law, and in 2001 he found that the Cayugas are entitled to an award of $247.9 million in total damages (*Cayuga Indian Nation of New York v. Pataki*, 165 F.Supp.2d 266 [N.D.N.Y. 2001]). However, the state of New York as well as two counties have filed appeals, and the Cayugas filed counter-appeals asking for $1.7 billion and all 64,027 acres. See Halftown, "The Haudenosaunee Cayuga Nation Land Claim"; Bob Herbert, "Justice, 200 Years Later," in *New York Times* (column, November 26, 2001); and David L. Shaw, "Settlement urged in Cayuga Claim," in *Syracuse Post Standard* (October 7, 2001).

19. One of the recommendations of the 1977 International NGO Conference on Discrimination Against Indigenous Populations in the Americas (see Notes, The Haudenosaunee: A Nation Since Time Immemorial, note 14 and accompanying text), to which this paper was originally presented, was "that the United Nations Special Committee on Decolonization hold hearings on all issues affecting Indigenous populations." See International NGO Conference on Discrimination against Indigenous Populations in the Americas, "*Programme of Actions*," in International Indian Treaty Council, *The Geneva Conference*, 22-24.

Sources

Books

Balsdon, J. P. V. D. *Rome: The Story of an Empire.* New York: McGraw Hill, 1970.

Barreiro, José ed. *Indian Roots of American Democracy.* Ithaka: Akwe:kon Press, Cornell University, 1992.

Belshaw, Cyril S. *Traditional Exchange and Modern Markets.* Eaglewood Cliffs: Prentice-Hall, Modernization of Traditional Societies Series, 1965.

Bilharz, Joy A. *The Allegany Senecas and Kinzua Dam: Forced Relocation through Two Generations.* Lincoln: University of Nebraska Press, 1998.

Brinton, Crane. *Civilization in the West: From the Old Stone Age To the Age of Louis XIV.* Eaglewood Cliffs: Prentice- Hall, 1973.

Campisi, Jack and Laurence M. Hauptman, eds. *The Oneida Indian Experience.* Syracuse: Syracuse University Press, 1988.

Carmer, Carl. *Dark Trees to the Wind: A Cycle of York State Years.* New York: David McKay Company, Inc., 1949.

Carnegie Institution of Washington, *European Treaties Bearing on the History of the Untied States and its Dependencies to 1648.* Washington, DC: Carnegie Institution of Washington, 1917.

Cohen, Felix S. *Handbook of Federal Indian Law.* Washington, DC: US Government Printing Office, 1942.

Deloria, Vine Jr. *Behind the Trail of Broken Treaties: An Indian Declaration of Independence.* New York: Dell Publishing, 1974.

Deloria, Vine Jr. and Clifford M. Lytle. *American Indians, American Justice.* Austin: University of Texas Press, 1988.

Deskaheh. *Chief Deskaheh Tells Why He Is Over Here Again* (pamphlet). London, August 1923.

Deskaheh. *The Redman's Appeal For Justice,* August 6, 1923, document submitted by Deskaheh to the League of Nations, file 33687/28075.

Ehle, John. *Trail of Tears: The Rise and Fall of the Cherokee Nation.* New York: Doubleday, 1988.

Engels, Frederick. *The Origin of the Family, Private Property and the State: In Light of the Researches of Lewis H. Morgan.* New York: International Publishers, 1972. Originally published 1884 in Hottingen-Zurich.

Freire, Paulo. *Pedagogy of the Oppressed.* New York: Continuum, 1970.

George-Kanentiio, Doug. *Iroquois Culture & Commentary.* Santa Fe: Clear Light Publishers, 2000.

Graymont, Barbara. *The Iroquois in the American Revolution.* Syracuse: Syracuse University Press, 1972.

Hanke, Louis. *The Spanish Struggle for Justice in the Conquest of America.* Philadelphia, Philadelphia: University of Philadelphia Press 1949.

Hauptman, Laurence M. *Conspiracy of Interests: Iroquois Dispossession and the Rise of New York State.* Syracuse: Syracuse University Press, 1999.

Hauptman, Laurence M. *The Iroquois and the New Deal.* Syracuse: Syracuse University Press, 1981.

Hauptman, Laurence M. *The Iroquois Struggle for Survival: World War II to Red Power.* Syracuse: Syracuse University Press, 1986.

Hauptman, Laurence M. *Tribes and Tribulations: Misconceptions about American Indians and Their Histories.* Albuquerque: University of New Mexico Press, 1995.

Hauptman, Laurence M. and L. Gordon McLester III, eds. *The Oneida Indian Journey: From New York to Wisconsin, 1784-1860.* Madison: University of Wisconsin Press, 1999.

Heiser, Charles B. Jr. *Seed to Civilization: the Story of Man's Food.* San Francisco: W.H. Freeman, 1973.

Hodges, Henry. *Technology in the Ancient World.* New York: Alfred Knopf, 1970.

International Work Group for Indigenous Affairs (IWGIA), *The Indigenous World 2001-2002.* Copenhagen: IWGIA, 2002.

Jaimes, M. Annette ed. *The State of Native America: Genocide, Colonization, and Resistance.* Boston: South End Press, 1992.

Jemison, G. Peter and Anna M. Schein, eds. *Treaty of Canandaigua 1794: 200 Years of Treaty Relations between the Iroquois Confederacy and the United States.* Santa Fe: Clear Light Publishers, 2000.

Jennings, Francis. *The Invasion of America: Indians, Colonialism, and the Cant of Conquest.* New York: W.W. Norton & Company, 1976.

Johansen, Bruce E. *Debating Democracy: Native American Legacy of Freedom.* Santa Fe: Clear Light Publishers, 1998.

Johansen, Bruce E. *Forgotten Founders: How the American Indian Helped Shape Democracy.* Harvard and Boston: The Harvard Common Press, 1982.

Johansen, Bruce E. and Barbara A. Mann, eds. *Encyclopedia of the Haudenosaunee (Iroquois Confederacy).* Westport: Greenwood Press, 2000.

Kroeber, Alfred L. *Anthropology: Race, Language, Culture, Psychology, Prehistory—Revised Edition.* New York: Harcourt, Brace and Company, 1948.

Landsman, Gail. *Sovereignty and Symbol: Indian-White Conflict at Ganienkeh.* Albuquerque: University of New Mexico Press, 1988.

Lyons, Oren R. *American Indian Sovereignty, Exiled in the Land of the Free.* Santa Fe: Clearlight Publishers, 1992.

Marx, Karl and Lawrence Krader, eds. *The Ethnological Notebooks of Karl Marx: Studies of Morgan, Phear, Maine, Lubbock.* Assen: Van Gorcum, 1972.

Morgan, Lewis Henry. *Ancient Society, or Researches in the Lines of Human Progress from Savagery, through Barbarism to Civilization.* London: Macmillan & Co., 1877.

Morgan, Lewis Henry. *League of the Ho-de'-no-sau-nee, or Iroquois.* Rochester: Sage & Brother, 1851.

National Lawyers Guild Committee on Native American Struggles, ed. *Rethinking Indian Law.* New Haven: The Advocate Press, 1982.

Newcomb, Steven. *A Matter of Religious Freedom.* Self-published essay, 1992.

Otis, Delos Sacket. *The Dawes Act and the Allotment of Indian Lands.* Norman: University of Oklahoma Press, 1973.

Purdue, Theda and Michael D. Green. *The Cherokee Removal: A Brief History with Documents.* New York: Bedford Books of St. Martin's Press, 1995.

Redfield, Margaret Park, ed. *Human Nature and the Study of Society: The Papers of Robert Redfield, Vol. 1.* Chicago: University of Chicago Press, 1962.

Redfield, Robert. *Peasant Society and Culture: An Anthropological Approach to Civilization.* Chicago: University of Chicago Press, 1956.

Rickard, Clinton. *Fighting Tuscarora: The Autobiography of Chief Clinton Rickard,* ed. Barbara Graymont. Syracuse: Syracuse University Press, 1973.

Sahlins, Marshall. *Stone Age Economics.* Chicago: Aldine Press, 1972.

Sauer, Carl O. *Agricultural Origins and Dispersals: The Domestication of Animals and Foodstuffs.* Cambridge: Massachusetts Institute of Technology Press, 1969.

Schaaf, Greg. *The Great Law of Peace and the Constitution of the United States of America.* Pamphlet published by Tree of Peace Society, 1987.

Shattuck, George C. *The Oneida Land Claims: A Legal History.* Syracuse: Syracuse University Press, 1991.

Taylor, Isaac. *Origin of the Aryans.* New York: Charles Scribner's Sons, 1895.

Tehanetorens. *Legends of the Iroquois.* Summertown, Tennessee: Book Publishng Company, 1998.

Tehanetorens. *Roots of the Iroquois.* Summertown, Tennessee: Native Voices, 2000.

Tehanetorens. *Sacred Song of the Hermit Thrush.* Summertown, Tennessee: Book Publishing Company, 1995.

Tehanetorens. *Wampum Belts of the Iroquois.* Summertown, Tennessee: Book Publishing Company, 1999.

Vecsey, Christopher and William A. Starna, eds. *Iroquois Land Claims.* Syracuse: Syracuse University Press, 1988.

Venne, Sharon H. *Our Elders Understand Our Rights: Evolving International Law Regarding Indigenous Rights.* Penticton: Theytus Books, Ltd., 1998.

Wagner, Sally Roesch. *Sisters in Spirit, Haudenosaunee (Iroquois) Influence on Early American Feminists.* Summertown, Tennessee: Native Voices, 2001.

Wallace, Anthony F. C. *The Death and Rebirth of the Seneca.* New York: Alfred A. Knopf, 1970.

Wallace, Paul. *White Roots of Peace: The Iroquois Book of Life.* Santa Fe: Clear Light Publishers, 1994.

White, Lynn, Jr., *Medieval Technology and Social Change.* Oxford: Oxford University Press, 1966.

Wolf, Eric R. *Peasants.* Eaglewood Cliffs: Prentice-Hall, Foundations of Modern Anthropology Series, 1966.

Articles, Periodicals, and Special Reports

Akwesasne Notes. Vol. 9, No. 5. December 1977.

Berkey, Curtis. "The Legal Basis for Iroquois Land Claims," in *Akwe:kon Journal* 10, No. 1 (Spring 1993), 23-25.

Carnegie Institution of Washington. *European Treaties Bearing on the History of the Untied States and its Dependencies to 1648.* Washington, DC: Carnegie Institution of Washington, 1917.

Halftown, Clint. "The Haudenosaunee Cayuga Nation Land Claim: Cayuga Nation v. New York," in *Buffalo Law Review* 46, No. 3 (Fall 1998), 1091-1095.

Hauptman, Laurence M. "Four Eastern New Yorkers and Seneca Lands: A Study in Treaty-Making," in *Hudson Valley Regional Review* 13 (March 1996), 1-19.

Hauptman, Laurence M. "Seneca Nation of Indians v. Christy: A Background Study," in *Buffalo Law Review* 46, No. 3 (Fall 1998), 947-979.

Hauptman, Laurence M. "The State's Men, the Salvation Seekers, and the Seneca: The Supplemental Treaty of Buffalo Creek, 1842," in *New York History* 78, No. 1 (January 1997), 51-116.

Herbert, Bob. "Justice, 200 Years Later," in *New York Times,* November 26, 2001.

Horn, Greg. "Ganienkeh celebrates 25th anniversary," in *The Eastern Door,* Vol. 8, No. 15 (May 7, 1999.

Horn, Greg. "Ganienkeh since 1977," in *The Eastern Door,* Vol. 8, No. 16 (May 14, 1999).

Institute for the Development of Indian Law. "International NGO Conference on Discrimination Against Indigenous Peoples–1977," in *American Indian Journal* 3 (1977).

International Indian Treaty Council. "The Geneva Conference: International NGO Conference On Discrimination Against Indigenous Populations–1977– In The Americas, September 20-23, Palais des Nations Geneva, Switzerland– Official Report by: International Indian Treaty Council" (Special Issue: *Treaty Council News,* October 1977, Vol. 1, No. 7).

Jacobs, Beverley K. (Assembly of First Nations–British Columbia). "The Effect of Delgamuukw on Treaties in Ontario" (January 2001. Research paper posted on the Delgamuukw/Gisday'wa National Process Web site, http://www.delgamuukw.org/research/ontariotreaties.pdf.

Manley, Henry S. "Buying Buffalo from the Indians," in *New York History* 27 (July 1947), 313-329.

Newcomb, Steven. "A Matter of Religious Freedom" Self-published essay 1992.

Powless, Chief Irving, Jr. "The Haudenosaunee, Yesterday and Today: A Conflict of Concepts and Laws," in *Buffalo Law Review* 46, No. 3 (Fall 1998), 1081-1090.

Shaw, David L. "Settlement urged in Cayuga Claim," in *Syracuse Post Standard,* October 7, 2001.

Sheffield, R. Scott. *A Search for Equity: A Study of the Treatment Accorded to First Nations Veterans and Dependents of the Second World War and the Korean Conflict* (April 2001). Report prepared for the National Roundtable on First Nations Veterans' Issues.

Tahsuda, John. "The Oneida Land Claim: Yesterday and Today," in *Buffalo Law Review* 46 No. 3 (Fall 1998), 1001-1009.

Washinawatok, Ingrid. "International Emergence: Twenty-One Years at the United Nations," in *New York City Law Review* 3 (1999), 41-57.

Woo, Grace Li Xiu. "Canada's Forgotten Founders: The Modern Significance of the Haudenosaunee (Iroquois) Application for Membership in the League of Nations," in *Law, Social Justice & Global Development Journal* (LGD) 2003 (1) (Coventry: University of Warwick, 2003), http://elj.warwick.ac.uk/global/issue /2003-1/woo.htm.

Government Publications

New York State Assembly, *Report of the Special Committee to Investigate the Indian Problem of the State of New York—Appointed by the Assembly of 1888*. Albany: Troy Press, 1889.

Royal Commission on Aboriginal Peoples, Report of the Royal Commission on Aboriginal Peoples. Ottawa: Canada Communication Group, 1996.

United States Congress Senate Select Committee On Indian Affairs Report 100-565, Acknowledging the Contribution of the Iroquois Confederacy of Nations To the Development of the United States Constitution. Washington, DC: US Government Printing Office, 1988.

Radio Broadcasts

Deskaheh, radio broadcast over station WHAM (Rochester, N.Y.), March 10, 1925.

Index

155

☞ Native Voices

tribal legends, medicine, arts & crafts,
history, life experiences, spirituality

Roots of the Iroquois

Tehanetorens

A vibrant, powerful democracy originated in North America long before the arrival of the Europeans. It grew out of a time of great warfare among the five Iroquois Nations. The Iroquois Confederacy that finally emerged was pledged to peace and controlled a territory large than the whole of Europe. Tehanetorens chronicles this pioneering experiment in government that stood as a model for the Post-Revolutionary American democracy.

1-54067-097-8   144 pages $9.95

Book Publishing Company • PO Box 99 • Summertown TN • 38483

☙ **Native Voices**

Legends of the Iroquois
Tehanetorens

Ancient stories are presented here in a unique way, using pictographs with English translations. These legends carry us deep into an ancient culture and teach basic lessons about what it means to be a human being. The pictographs are intriguing for both children and adults.

"A treasured contribution to Native American literature." *Wisconsin Bookwatch*

978-1-57067-056-5   *112 pages*   *$9.95*

Wampum Belts of the Iroquois
Tehanetorens

The history of the Iroquois Confederacy, its treaties, the deaths of chiefs, and important events in the life of its people are written in patterned beadwork called wampum belts. Many photos of Native children holding traditional belts.

978-1-57067-082-4   *96 pages*   *$9.95*

Sisters in Spirit
Iroquois   Influence   on   Early American Feminists
Sally Roesch Wagner

A recount of the compelling history of women's struggle for freedom and equality in this country and a documentation of the Iroquois influence on this broad social movement.

978-1-57067-121-0   *128 pages*   *$11.95*

Book Publishing Company • PO Box 99 • Summertown TN • 38483
1-888-260-8458• *Please add $3.95 per book.*

7th Generation *publications celebrate the stories and achievements of Native people in North America through fiction and biography.*

The NATIVE TRAILBLAZER *series for adolescent readers provides positive role models of Native men and women whose lives have had a positive impact in their communities and beyond.*

For more information, visit **nativevoicesbooks.com**

Native Writers:
Voices of Power

Kimberly Sigafus and Lyle Ernst
978-0-97791-838-6 • $9.95

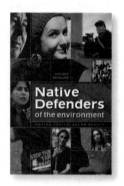

Native Defenders
of the Environment

Vincent Schilling
978-0-97791-837-9 • $9.95

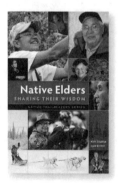

Native Elders:
Sharing Their Wisdom

Kimberly Sigafus and Lyle Ernst
978-0-97791-836-2 • $9.95

Native Musicians
in the Groove

Vincent Schilling
978-0-97791-834-8 • $9.95

Available from your local bookstore or you can buy them directly from:
Book Publishing Company • PO Box 99 • Summertown, TN 38483
888-260-8458 • *Please include $3.95 per book for shipping and handling.*